PARIS: BIRTHPLACE OF THE U.S.A.

Writer:
DANIEL JOUVE
Editor:
ALICE JOUVE
Art Director:
ALVIN GROSSMAN

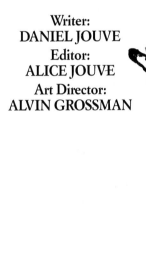

Gründ

60, rue Mazarine
75006 Paris

PARIS:
BIRTHPLACE
OF THE
U.S.A.

A Walking Guide For The American Patriot

TABLE OF CONTENTS

This book is long overdue. Unconsciously, I have been waiting for many years for Daniel Jouve—or someone like him—to write it. I am now totally delighted to possess *Paris: Birthplace of the U.S.A.*

Let me tell you why.

"France is the United States of America's oldest friend." A cliché perhaps, but certainly a fact whose accuracy has never been questioned.

France's prompt and generous support of the American Revolution—with moral suasion, men, materiel, and money—was a crucial factor in establishing my country's independence. Rochambeau, La Fayette, Washington, Franklin—are names which are inter-related very early in the academic life of every American student.

Recent generations on both sides of the Atlantic are sentimentally alert to the close French-American alliances in two World Wars, in the Gulf War, and, over the years, in other strategic missions in defense of democracy. There is also general familiarity, among the French and the Americans, with the more prominent dimples and warts of each other's national peculiarities.

The lines between the U.S. and France have always been historically tight—whether it be in matters relating to the philosophy of freedom, or to culture, trade and commerce, or war and peace.

For two centuries Americans of all stripes have come to France, and have been gripped, exhilarated, and seduced by certain aspects of the Gallic mystique; they have also been challenged and bewildered by other things in France. But there has always been the exciting fact that repeated waves of us have been inspired and transcended by France—and, perhaps particularly, by Paris, the Siren of Sirens.

The traces of American expatriates, refugees, heroes and rascals are discoverable throughout this city. But the ones of most compelling interest to Daniel Jouve are those, with their French counterparts, who were specifically pertinent to the birth of a newly independent country in North America.

It has been a rather elite secret about where these extraordinary characters have left their vibrations in Paris. The average French or American citizen is usually unaware—indeed oblivious—of these places that featured, in various ways, in the achievement of American independence.

Daniel Jouve—a man for all seasons and many disciplines, prodded by great affection for both countries, and in close collaboration with his American, Boston-bred wife Alice—has fashioned a unique key to these special places. Thanks to the scholarship and editorial flair of Alice Jouve and to the passionate sleuthing of her husband, an American patriot of any age can set off on foot, sustained by a robust curiosity and a copy of *Paris: Birthplace of the U.S.A.*, to rediscover the sites where the essence of French complicity in the founding of my country lingers on.

For the readers' further pleasure, Alvin Grossman, the Art Director, has created a beautiful volume that appeals to the best of French and American tastes.

One of my early predecessors, Thomas Jefferson, reflecting on his term as U.S. Ambassador to France and upon his long admiration for the country, its people, and its capital, said: "---A walk about Paris will provide lessons in history, in beauty, and in the point of Life." Daniel and Alice Jouve seem to agree.

Take a walk with them. You will never forget it.

Walter J.P. Curley
U.S. Ambassador to France (1989–1993)
    and to Ireland (1975–1977)
July 4, 1994
Paris

INTRODUCTION

This book deals with American history, but it is also a guide book for those who like to walk through the streets of Paris and feel that it is exciting to open the same doors, climb the same steps, and touch the same walls that the Founding Fathers did.

The map in the back of the book indicates the twenty-three places described in each of the chapters. There is no obligation to visit the places in a specific order although they have been listed almost chronologically.

The two most important sites are the Hotel de Coislin (chapter two) and the Hotel d'York[1] (chapter nine). They justify the title of the book: *Paris: Birthplace of the U.S.A.* It was at the Hotel de Coislin that France, first of all nations, recognized the independence of the United States in 1778. It was at the Hotel d'York that England recognized the independence of her former colonies in 1783. All the other places will tell you about the people and the events related to this important moment in history.

Obviously, this book is centered on Paris and the French connections with American independence. Readers who already have visited the sites of the War of Independence in their own country will find a complement to their knowledge on this side of the Atlantic Ocean.

From time to time, nationalistic historians or disgruntled politicians, both French and American, love to say that if France was involved in the War of Independence, it was to pursue her own self-interest.

True, "la raison d'Etat" existed and France was not going to forget where its interest lay. Reading the testimonies of the time, however, would convince anybody of the tremendous emotional support for the American cause that came from every part of French society.

- Many aristocrats volunteered for the war and served with the American forces even before France officially went to war in 1778. La Fayette was one of many...

- The King of France secretly supplied the Insurgents with money from the Royal Treasury to buy weapons and equipment.

- Collections were taken up in the streets of Paris to pay for the flagship of de Grasse's fleet, the "Ville de Paris."

- Ladies at the Court of Versailles collected money to buy a battleship for John Paul Jones.

- French officers fought to get on board ships leaving for America. The future Maréchal Alexandre Berthier was one of them.

- The Insurgents were so popular that they inspired the fashion of the times. Marie-Antoinette wore a hat "à la John Paul Jones." There were coats "à l'Insurgente," and dresses called "Lightning Conductor" to honor Franklin. Hairstyles were "à la Boston, à la Philadelphie." A new coiffure "aux Insurgents" was all the more popular because it was forbidden by law! Everyone liked hats, gloves, and snuff boxes "à la Benjamin Franklin."

- Even the most cynical and critical French writer of the century, Voltaire, became enthusiastic about the American cause. He rooted for Doctor Franklin's armies! And, for once, he wrote praises...praises for the Americans:

"Chaque peuple à son tour a brillé sur la terre,
Par les lois, par les arts, et surtout par la
   guerre.
Le temps de l'Amérique est à la fin venu.
Ce peuple généreux, trop longtemps inconnu
Laissait dans les déserts ensevelir sa gloire:
Voici les jours nouveaux marqués par la
   victoire."

Each Nation in time has shined on the world
Through its laws, its arts and mostly by war.
America's time has come.
This generous nation unknown for too long
Was allowing its glory to be buried in its deserts.
A new day has risen marked by victory.

The American people did not forget and named their new cities for Louis XVI (Louisville, Kentucky), Marie-Antoinette (Marietta, Georgia & Ohio), Vergennes (Vermont), but they went overboard with their darling La Fayette: forty-four cities and thirty-seven counties bear his name!

Research for this book was begun with *Americans in Paris, an anecdotal street guide,* the Olivia and Hill Press, Ann Harbor, Michigan, 1984, and *American Footprints in Paris.* George H. Doran Company, New York, 1921.

[1] *Through this guidebook the word "hotel" is used many times with different meanings. A hotel is a residence and most of the time the word hotel is followed by the name of the family which built it or lived in it. Often the name of the family stays even if the hotel is sold. Sometimes it means simply a hotel for travellers. It is even used for large institutions like Hôtel des Invalides which means official residence for invalid veterans.*

HOTEL DES AMBASSADEURS DE HOLLANDE

Roderigue Hortalez & Cie — Caron de Beaumarchais
47, rue Vieille du Temple, Paris 4e
MÉTRO: **Hôtel de Ville or Saint Paul**

This imposing seventeenth-century mansion was once the headquarters of Pierre-Áuguste Caron de Beaumarchais. (Ring to see the courtyard—the house is not open to the public.) It was here that Beaumarchais operated a fictitious trading company named Roderigue Hortalez & Cie. Through this company the king of France, Louis XVI, and his Minister of Foreign Affairs, the Comte de Vergennes, secretly channeled arms, ammunition, and uniforms to the American Insurgents at a time when France was still officially at peace with England.

Born Pierre-Auguste Caron in 1732, Beaumarchais was a man of many talents. Son of a clockmaker (a lowly origin that French aristocrats enjoyed reminding him of), he became clockmaker to Louis XV, then music tutor to his daughters. He rapidly climbed the social ladder at Versailles and was named secretary to the king in 1761. The position brought him a title; and, thereafter, he called himself Caron de Beaumarchais. Louis XVI sent him as a secret agent to London where he became enthusiastic about the cause of American independence. He shared this enthusiasm with Vergennes who saw great opportunities for trade with the potential new country.

However, Vergennes and his twenty-year-old king hesitated to help the Americans openly because they were not yet ready to take on a war with England. The Finance Minister, Turgot, cautioned that a war would create too much burden on the French bugdet.

Beaumarchais' eloquence finally prevailed. Louis XVI and Vergennes decided to supply the Insurgents secretly with 1,000,000 *livres* from the Royal Treasury in June 1776. Louis XVI convinced his cousin, Charles III of Spain, to offer the same amount. The money was to be channeled through the fictitious Roderigue Hortalez & Cie. to buy arms and equipment. Beaumarchais would be responsible for its delivery to the Americans. No one was to suspect Louis XVI's hand in the operation. At the same time, Congress sent an envoy to Paris in the hope of negotiating help from Vergennes. A Connecticut school-master turned merchant and Congressman, Silas Deane, arrived in Paris in July 1776. He signed a contract with Beaumarchais to buy arms and equipment for 30,000 men to be paid for by Congress at a later date.

From the fall of 1776 to early 1778, the courtyard of this elegant town house fairly bristled with activity. Beaumarchais hired thirty people to deal with the arms and ammunition that passed through the company, while, he, himself, moved into an apartment on the first floor. Dodging British spies, he and Deane travelled to Nantes, Bordeaux and Le Havre to supervise the loading of a fleet of ships that Beaumarchais had chartered with his own money. The ships also carried the first French artillery officers, travelling under false passports, and volunteers who wanted to help the Insurgents. Among the passengers were Baron Frederick Wilhelm von Steuben, who brought discipline to the American troops, and Pierre L'Enfant, engineer and volunteer, who later designed the new American capital, Washington, D.C.

In January 1777, a second secret loan of 2,000,000 *livres* was granted by Louis XVI. Things were going so well that the indefatigable Beaumarchais even found time to continue his career as a playwright. After the success of the *Barber of Seville* in 1775, he began writing the *Marriage of Figaro*.

When the news of the first decisive American victory arrived in Paris in December 1777, "Beaumarchais l'Americain," as he enjoyed being called, could be justly proud that the arms and supplies he sent were responsible for the defeat of General Burgoyne at Saratoga. This victory was a turning point in the War of Independence. Encouraged by the American victory, Louis XVI and Vergennes decided to collaborate openly with the new-born nation.

Payment for the arms and supplies, however, was the source of long discussions in Congress who finally repaid Beaumarchais 2,500,000 *livres* in 1782. Beaumarchais esteemed that he was owed much more, for he had invested most of his personal fortune in the enterprise. It was only in 1835, thirty-six years after his death, that Congress finally voted to pay 800,000 francs to his heirs!

A statue of Beaumarchais can be found in the small square at the corner of rue Saint-Antoine and rue des Tournelles, near place de la Bastille.

2

HOTEL DE COISLIN

**Treaties of Friendship, Commerce and Alliance.
Independence of the U.S.A. recognized by France.
4, place de la Concorde, Paris 8e
MÉTRO: Concorde**

It is in this building, on February 6, 1778 that the United States of America joined the community of free, independent states. That day, a small group of Americans and French gathered in Silas Deane's apartment on the second floor of the Hôtel de Coislin at the corner of rue Royale and place de la Concorde (then, Place Louis XV). They signed the Treaties of Friendship, Commerce and Alliance by which France, first of all nations, recognized the independence of the United States. Conrad Alexandre Gerard represented the King of France. The American delegates were Benjamin Franklin, Silas Deane and Arthur Lee.

Until that moment, the American nation, born in the thirteen colonies and unified in the Declaration of Independence of 1776, did not exist as an independent country, nor did it have official ambassadors. Its citizens were not recognized abroad or protected by a consul. For the rest of the world, Americans were still subjects of the British monarch. On this fateful day, one of the major powers in Europe recognized the independence of the United States of America.

The treaty provided that France would not lay down her arms until the independence of the United States was achieved, and that the Americans would fight on the side of France if England declared war. It further provided that neither party would seek a separate peace, and each granted the other the trading status of most favored nation. Finally, both countries swore to eternal peace between them.

The signing of the treaty marked the success of Franklin's long, patient efforts to win France's help since his arrival in Paris in December 1776. For the

★   ★

EN CET HOTEL
LE 6 FEVRIER 1778
CONRAD A. GERARD
AU NOM DE LOUIS XVI, ROI DE FRANCE
BENJAMIN FRANKLIN
SILAS DEANE, ARTHUR LEE,
AU NOM DES ETATS-UNIS D'AMERIQUE
ONT SIGNE LES TRAITES
D'AMITIE, DE COMMERCE ET D'ALLIANCE
PAR LESQUELS LA FRANCE,
AVANT TOUTE AUTRE NATION,
RECONNAISSAIT L'INDEPENDANCE
DES ETATS-UNIS

IN THIS BUILDING
ON FEBRUARY 6TH 1778
CONRAD A. GERARD,
IN THE NAME OF LOUIS XVI, KING OF FRANCE
BENJAMIN FRANKLIN
SILAS DEANE, ARTHUR LEE
ON BEHALF OF THE UNITED STATES
SIGNED THE TREATIES
OF FRIENDSHIP, COMMERCE AND ALLIANCE,
BY WHICH FRANCE,
FIRST OF ALL NATIONS,
RECOGNIZED THE INDEPENDENCE
OF THE UNITED STATES

★   ★

British Ambassador, Lord Stormont, whose spies had kept track of the wily septuagenarian's every movement, it was a major setback. News of the treaty was rushed to England. When the British arrived to negotiate with the Colonies, they found that the Franco-American treaty had already been ratified by Congress.

The importance of the treaty can hardly be under-estimated. France's recognition of the United States was certainly a bold move. The American government did not even control its territory: New York was occupied by British troops. Furthermore, a large number of American loyalists, estimated at 50% of the population, were against independence and faithful to the king of England.

The most famous of them was William Franklin, illegitimate son of Benjamin and father of William Temple Franklin, who accompanied his grandfather to Paris. William Franklin became the royal governor of New Jersey. In 1776, he was accused of treason and put in jail. Liberated through an exchange of prisoners, he became President of the Loyalists and left for Great Britain in 1782.

On May 20th, as Louis XVI was receiving the American delegation with great ceremony at Versailles, the British Ambassador was recalled to London. Hostilities were about to begin in earnest.

Jefferson's silversmith, Odiot, can still be found just a short walk down the elegant rue Royale on 7, place de la Madeleine (chapter 12 page 56).

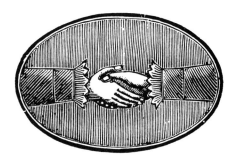

3

CIMETIERE DE PICPUS

La Fayette's grave.
35, rue de Picpus, Paris 12e
METRO: Picpus

Marie Joseph Paul Roch Yves Gilbert Motier, Marquis de La Fayette, was buried here on May 20, 1834 at the age of seventy-seven.

La Fayette first heard about the American struggle for independence while stationed in Metz as a French army officer in 1776. Young and idealistic, he immediately resolved to serve the American cause of liberty. Early in 1777, he signed an agreement with Silas Deane to serve as a major general in the Continental Army. He bought a ship, which he named "La Victoire" and equipped it at his own expense. However, a wealthy young man with a high profile at the Court of Versailles could not take up the American cause without endangering official French neutrality, and Louis XVI issued an order to prevent his departure. Deterred neither by his family nor his king, La Fayette left for America in the utmost secrecy from a small Spanish port in April 1777.

He reached South Carolina in mid-June and rode 600 miles to Philadelphia to present his credentials to the Continental Congress. A skeptical Congress first denied his application as coming from just another foreigner who expected a commission in the U.S. Army. They soon realized, however, that La Fayette was in a class by himself. Captivated by his enthusiasm for their cause and his wish to serve without pay, Congress decided to give him the rank of Major General — one month before his twentieth birthday. Soon after, La Fayette met General Washington, who took an instant liking to him. He adopted La Fayette as the son he never had, while La Fayette found in his General the father he had lost in battle.

La Fayette proved to be a brave and capable officer who learned quickly. He arrived at a time when the American army, lacking food, clothing, and materiel was ill-equipped to overcome the superior British forces commanded by General Howe. Moreover, the British Fleet was the overwhelming master of the seas.

★ ★

M.J.P.R.Y.G.D.
LA FAYETTE
LIEUTENANT GENERAL
MEMBRE DE LA CHAMBRE DES DEPUTES
NE A CHAVANIAC HAUTE LOIRE
LE VI SEPTEMBRE MDCCLVII
MARIE LE XI AVRIL MDCCLXXIV
A
M.A.F. DE NOAILLES

★ ★

With New York securely in British hands and General Burgoyne on his way south from Canada via the Hudson in an attempt to isolate New England, Howe decided to march on Philadelphia. He met Washington's forces in September at Brandywine. The Americans were defeated once again and La Fayette was wounded. After being hospitalized for a month, he rejoined Washington to share the hardships of the terrible winter at Valley Forge. Washington had not prevented Howe from occupying Philadelphia as Congress fled to Baltimore, but La Fayette was rewarded for his bravery with the command of an infantry division.

There was, however, some cheering news. Burgoyne had been defeated at Saratoga in October. The news of the American victory was enough to convince France to sign a treaty of alliance with the United States. Louis XVI promised to send a fleet of ships and 4000 soldiers commanded by Admiral d'Estaing. Hearing this news, the British evacuated Philadelphia for the safety of New York. General Howe was replaced by General Clinton.

July 1778 found La Fayette leading two crack brigades under General Sullivan in an attempt to dislodge the British from Newport, Rhode Island. A combined operation was planned with the newly-arrived French fleet. Unfortunately, a British fleet came to challenge d'Estaing, and a severe gale drove both fleets off course. The joint operation collapsed, and the local militia left for home!

That winter, La Fayette returned to France to promote the American cause. He was received as a hero at the Court which was flattered by the attention he had received in America. Moved by La Fayette's impassioned pleas, Louis XVI agreed to send 6000 men under General Rochambeau to help the Americans. In the spring of 1780, La Fayette brought the good news to Washington who put him in command of 1200 of his best soldiers, the Light Cavalry. On his return, La Fayette discovered that the British had successfully moved the war to the south which had been largely spared by violence up until that time. Early in 1779, the British had occupied Georgia, and a joint operation with Admiral d'Estaing had failed to rout the enemy from Savannah. D'Estaing had returned to France without having accomplished anything.

In the spring of 1780, General Clinton, who had sailed from New York with a huge expeditionary force, had taken the South Carolina port of Charleston and had left General Cornwallis in command. Cornwallis quickly moved north into North Carolina and Virginia. Washington's efforts to contain him were fruitless. Late in 1780, he dispatched La Fayette with his elite troops to take command of the army in Virginia.

It wasn't until the following June, however, that La Fayette received the necessary reinforcement that enabled him to march 5000 strong from Fredricks-burg to Williamsburg.

It was at that moment that General Clinton, fearing the arrival of a new French fleet under Admiral de Grasse, ordered Cornwallis to hold the seaport at Yorktown for the British fleet. Cornwallis moved his army to Yorktown early in August and began to fortify the town. La Fayette occupied nearby Williamsburg while he awaited the arrival of Washington's and Rochambeau's troops by land and de Grasse's fleet by sea.

After the decisive victory of the French and American forces at Yorktown in October, La Fayette returned to France in December 1781 where he continued to lead an active career in public life. During the French Revolution, he was Commander of the National Guard. Exiled and jailed at Olmutz by the Austrians, he was released in 1797 upon protests of the American government. Out of office under Napoleon, he came back as a member of Parliament from 1818 to 1824. Later, he convinced the revolutionaries of 1830, who overthrew the last king of France, Charles X, to choose Louis-Philippe d'Orléans as king of the French.

La Fayette returned twice to the United States after the War. In 1784, he toured the battlefields, and stayed with Washington at Mount Vernon. Acclaimed in all the major cities of the East Coast, La Fayette was, at twenty-eight, the "Hero of Two Worlds." La Fayette's farewell visit took place in 1824. At the invitation of Congress, he was a "guest of the Nation" for an entire year. Together with his son, George Washington La Fayette, the sixty-seven-year-old Marquis visited all twenty-four states. He was deeply moved by the tremendous outpouring of gratitude of the American people wherever he went. He was made an honorary citizen of the United States, and his descendants still have the right to carry an American passport.

When La Fayette's wife, Adrienne de Noailles, died in 1807, she asked to be buried in the private cemetery of Picpus next to the other members of her family who had been victims of the Terror during the French Revolution. They had been buried here in a common grave along with 1300 victims of the guillotine in 1793 and 1794. La Fayette was buried beside her in soil that he brought back from America in 1824.

On July 4, 1917, General Pershing came to visit La Fayette's grave and, after his speech, his deputy Colonel Stanton declared: "La Fayette, we are here!"

Today, every 4th of July, U.S. officials, French Cincinnati Society members, and French Sons of the Revolution gather to remember La Fayette. A Star Spangled Banner always flies over the grave. During World War II, it was the only American flag in occupied Paris.

October 15th to April 14th open 2 p.m. to 4 p.m. (except Sunday & Monday).
April 15th to October 14th open 2 p.m. to 6 p.m. (except Monday).
Closed from July 14th to August 15th.
Tel 01.43.44.18.54.

★★★

Hôtel St. James and Albany, ex-Hôtel de Noailles, 202, rue de Rivoli, Paris 1er. Reach the courtyard through the lobby. This magnificent mansion was Madame de La Fayette's family residence. La Fayette was often a guest here. It is in the chapel of this residence that the Marquis and his wife Adrienne de Noailles were married on April 11, 1774. The Marquis was only 17 but had been engaged to Adrienne three years earlier. He was then 14, and his bride-to-be, just 12! After the wedding, he joined the family like an extra child and continued his studies until he left for military school.

In the courtyard, a plaque reads:

DANS CET HOTEL
EUT LIEU
LE 15 FEVRIER 1779
L'ENTREVUE DU
GENERAL LA FAYETTE
A SON RETOUR D'AMERIQUE
AVEC LA REINE
MARIE-ANTOINETTE

8, rue d'Anjou, Paris 8e. In 1827, La Fayette rented the second-floor apartment overlooking the courtyard of this eighteenth-century town house. He died here on May 20, 1834. The building is unchanged, and a plaque on the facade reads:

LE GENERAL
LA FAYETTE
DEFENSEUR DE LA LIBERTE
EN AMERIQUE
UN DES FONDATEURS
DE LA LIBERTE EN FRANCE
NE LE 4 SEPTEMBRE 1757
AU CHATEAU DE CHAVAGNAC
EN AUVERGNE
EST MORT DANS CETTE MAISON
LE 20 MAI 1834

4

JOHN PAUL JONES' RESIDENCE

19, rue de Tournon, Paris 6e
MÉTRO: Mabillon or Odéon

John Paul Jones, founder of the U.S. Navy, moved into the third floor of this building in 1789. He died lonely and penniless at the age of forty-five on July 18, 1792.

The American Ambassador to Paris at the time, Gouverneur Morris, refused to spend money on his funeral and even to attend. Outraged, the French National Assembly voted for a state funeral with full honors.

The French, knowing that one day America would choose to remember their hero, preserved his body in a sealed lead coffin filled with alcohol and buried him in the Protestant Cemetery of Paris. That day came in 1905. Theodore Roosevelt decided to have his body brought back to Annapolis where it now rests in the crypt of the Naval Academy Chapel. His coffin, escorted by 500 U.S. Navy men, was taken to the American Cathedral on avenue Georve V (then, avenue de l'Alma), down the Champs Elysées, out to Cherbourg and across the Atlantic on the "S.S. Brooklyn."

John Paul Jones was one of the most colorful heroes of the War of Independence. Born in Scotland in 1747, he settled in America in the early 1770's.

When Congress founded the Continental Navy in October 1775, Jones, a seaman since the age of thirteen, was one of the first officers to be recruited. Soon, he was commanding his own ship off the New England coast. Then Washington decided that Jones would be more useful raiding English waters and sent him to France in November 1777.

Early in 1778, the intrepid Jones set sail for the British Isles in the "Ranger," raiding ports and capturing ships. In 1779, Franklin used his influence to find him a new ship, an old East Indiaman, which Jones renamed the "Bonhomme Richard" in honor of Franklin's *Poor Richard's Almanac.*

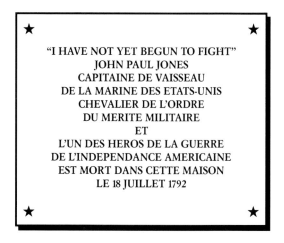

★ ★

"I HAVE NOT YET BEGUN TO FIGHT"
JOHN PAUL JONES
CAPITAINE DE VAISSEAU
DE LA MARINE DES ETATS-UNIS
CHEVALIER DE L'ORDRE
DU MERITE MILITAIRE
ET
L'UN DES HEROS DE LA GUERRE
DE L'INDEPENDANCE AMERICAINE
EST MORT DANS CETTE MAISON
LE 18 JUILLET 1792

★ ★

Commanding a small fleet of mostly French ships under the American flag, Jones set sail around the British Isles. On September 23, 1779, he fought the greatest battle of his career in the North Sea and captured the fifty-gun British warship, "HMS Serapis". In a fierce battle lasting into the night, Jones continued to fight from his disabled ship long after any other captain would have surrendered. The British admiral, thinking that Jones was ready to surrender, called, "Have you struck your flag?" "I have not yet begun to fight," bellowed Jones. In the end, it was the British admiral who surrendered his sword. The "Bonhomme Richard" was so badly damaged that it sank immediately, and Jones, transferring his flag to the "Serapis," sailed safely back to port.

Back in Paris, Jones received a hero's welcome, especially from the ladies. Marie-Antoinette received him at Versailles, but it was to his greatest admirer in Paris, the Duchess of Orléans, that he offered the sword he had captured from the British admiral.

Abigail Adams, who entertained Jones at her home in Paris, had expected to meet a raw-boned sailor but was pleasantly surprised. "He is of small stature, well-proportioned, soft in his speech, easy in his address, polite in his manner, vastly civil, understands all the etiquette of a lady's toilette as perfectly as he does the mast, sails and rigging of his ship!" she wrote. As Jones was eager to learn French, Benjamin Franklin advised him to learn with a "sleeping dictionary." Franklin's hostess in Passy, Madame de Chaumont, was only too happy to oblige him!

Jones returned to America, but soon was sent back to Paris after the peace treaty of 1783 to settle the difficulties concerning captured vessels. Later, he was called to Russia where he was named Vice Admiral of the Russian fleet by Catherine II. He did not get along with Field Marshall Potemkine, however, and returned to Paris.

John Paul Jones was admired not only by the French ladies, but by all Frenchmen. Louis XVI honored him with a gold sword and the Cross of Military Merit. Houdon sculpted his portrait. The people of Paris mourned his death. Even Napoleon, after his cruel defeat at Trafalgar, said of him: "If John Paul Jones had lived, France would have had an Admiral!"

On the ground floor, Librairie Thomas-Scheler deals in rare books and documents, some of which concern American history.

5

ROCHAMBEAU'S RESIDENCE

**Rochambeau. French chapter of the Cincinnati
Society founded here
40, rue du Cherche-Midi, Paris 6e
METRO: Sèvres-Babylone**

This building was once the home of General Jean-Baptiste Donatien de Vimeur, Comte de Rochambeau. One wintry day in February 1780, as this fifty-five-year-old professional soldier was preparing to leave for his country estate to enjoy a well-deserved retirement, a knock at the door brought the king's messenger. To his great astonishment, Rochambeau was being called back to command the troops that Louis XVI was sending to help the American colonies.

On May 2nd, a huge fleet of ships crammed with 5000 soldiers and officers, artillery, and supplies left Brest for America. It was a logistical "tour de force" for the time. Even at that, several thousand soldiers had to be left behind for lack of vessels to carry them. They endured a seventy-two-day crossing, dodging British warships sent to intercept them, and finally arrived at Newport, Rhode Island on July 11.

On arriving in Newport, Rochambeau immediately placed himself under the orders of General Washington. The two generals met in Hartford half-way between Newport and Washington's headquarters outside New York, but wisely decided that any attack on the British position in New York would be disastrous without the help of a naval fleet. At the time, the British fleet was unopposed. They had already blockaded Rochambeau in Newport, although the French artillery positions had made the port secure.

JEAN BAPTISTE DONATIEN
DE VIMEUR
COMTE DE ROCHAMBEAU
MARECHAL DE FRANCE
1725 - 1807
HABITAIT CET HOTEL
QUAND IL RECUT LE
COMMANDEMENT DE
L'ARMEE ENVOYEE PAR
LE ROI LOUIS XVI
EN AMERIQUE, 1780,
POUR AIDER LES
ETATS-UNIS A CONQUERIR
LEUR INDEPENDANCE

LA SECTION FRANCAISE
DE LA
SOCIETE DES CINCINNATI
A ETE
FONDEE DANS CET HOTEL
7 - 16 JANVIER 1784
EN SOUVENIR DE LA GUERRE
DE L'INDEPENDANCE
AMERICAINE

The people of Newport were, at first, wary of Rochambeau's 4000 men quartered in the town. Rochambeau soon won their admiration as he was determined not to be a burden on the population. His men paid for all their supplies, rented their winter quarters, and observed the strictest discipline. The population was amazed to see that never a chicken disappeared from the barnyard, nor an apple from the trees. The young ladies in the town were charmed by the gallantry of the French officers who represented some of the finest noble families of France. President Stiles of Yale University overcame the language barrier while dining with Rochambeau by conversing in Latin!

The following spring, Washington and Rochambeau were encouraged by the news that Admiral de Grasse had left Brest for the West Indies in March with a fleet of twenty warships, and that he was planning to be in American waters in midsummer.

On June 9, Rochambeau's four regiments, a battalion of artillery, and the Duke of Lauzun's celebrated Cavalry Legion set out from Newport to join Washington's army on the Hudson. Both generals observed Clinton's fortifications in New York, but decided that any attempt to attack would be futile. It was at that moment, on August 14, that a message announced de Grasse's arrival in the Chesapeake at the end of the month.

Reluctantly giving up his project of capturing New York, Washington bowed to the wisdom of Rochambeau's reasoning and de Grasse's decision that the key place to engage in battle against the British was in the Chesapeake. Washington, however, feared the insurmountable difficulties of moving his war-torn soldiers 400 miles to the south with hardly enough to eat or wear. Nevertheless, he set out on August 19 with his 2000 men, accompanied by Rochambeau's force of 4000.

By early September, the French, dressed in impeccable uniforms and plumed hats, passed in review before Congress and the French minister to the delight of the people of Philadelphia, On September 18, all the troops had reached La Fayette at Williamsburg as the net tightened slowly around Cornwallis at Yorktown.

After the victory at Yorktown in October, Rochambeau remained with his men in Virginia until the following June. Assured that peace was at hand, Rochambeau said farewell to his troops and to his friend General Washington, and returned to France in January 1783. The "Founding Father," as some American historians think he should be called, was considered a hero.

It was in this building, still the Rochambeau residence, that the officers of the French army who had served in America, gathered in 1784 to create the French chapter of the Society of Cincinnati. That patriotic society was founded in 1783 by the American officers who had fought in the War of Independence and who modeled themselves after the Roman hero Cincinnatus.

Two doors away to the left at number 44 is the house where Abbé Grégoire lived and died. In 1787, he was one of the founders of the French Society of the Friends of the Blacks (chapter 22 page 85). He later became one of the leading figures of the French Revolution.

6

EGLISE SAINT-ROCH

Tomb of Admiral de Grasse
Opposite 193/195, rue Saint-Honoré, Paris ler
METRO: Tuileries or Pyramides

Open 8 a.m. to 7 p.m.
Tel 01.42.44.13.20.

François-Joseph-Paul de Grasse was born in Grasse in southern France in 1722 and was trained as a naval officer in the order of Malta. A sailor since the age of twelve, de Grasse had seen forty-seven years of active duty and had the reputation of being one of the French Royal Navy's finest tacticians when Louis XVI called on him to help the Americans.

When de Grasse set sail from Brest in March 1781, the U.S. cause was at its lowest ebb. Even the combined French and American forces were powerless because the British controlled the sea and all the ports along the American coast. Mindful of earlier failures to dislodge the British in 1778 and 1779, Louis XVI decided this time to commit the best part of the Royal Navy. De Grasse commanded a powerful fleet of twenty-eight ships from his flagship "Ville de Paris." The 120-gun, three-deck ship was the pride of the French Royal Navy.

After sending Admiral de Barras to Newport with a message for Rochambeau, de Grasse went first to the West Indies to defend the interests of the French colonies there. Early in June, the frigate "Concorde" brought him a message from Rochambeau and Washington, detailing the problems that the allied forces faced both in New York and in Virginia. De Grasse replied that he would be most useful to their case in the defense of the Chesapeake where Cornwallis' troops had concentrated.

De Grasse then took on more ships, embarked 3,200 soldiers under the command of Marquis de Saint Simon, and borrowed 1,500,000 *Livres* from the Spanish in Havana. He sailed north on August 13 with the British Admiral Hood in hot pursuit.

A LA MEMOIRE DU COMTE DE GRASSE

L'AN MIL SEPT CENT QUATRE-VINGT HUIT, LE SEIZE JANVIER,
A ETE INHUME EN CETTE EGLISE LE CORPS DE
FRANCOIS-JOSEPH PAUL, COMTE DE GRASSE, MARQUIS DE TILLY
DES PRINCES D'ANTIBES,
LIEUTENANT GENERAL DES ARMEES NAVALES,
COMMANDEUR DE L'ORDRE ROYAL ET MILITAIRE DE SAINT-LOUIS
CHEVALIER DE L'ORDRE DE SAINT-JEAN DE JERUSALEM,
MEMBRE DE LA SOCIETE DES CINCINNATI,
NE AU CHATEAU DU BAR, PRES GRASSE, LE 13 SEPTEMBRE 1722.
DECEDE A PARIS, LE 14 JANVIER 1788.
PAR LA VICTOIRE NAVALE QU'IL REMPORTA SUR LES ANGLAIS A LA CHESAPEAKE
LE 5 SEPTEMBRE 1781, LE COMTE DE GRASSE RENDIT POSSIBLE LA
CAPITULATION DE YORKTOWN, ASSIEGE PAR L'ARMEE FRANCO-AMERICAINE
SOUS LES ORDRES DU GENERAL WASHINGTON
ET DU LIEUTENANT GENERAL COMTE DE DE ROCHAMBEAU, AINSI IL ACQUIT AVEC EUX
LA GLOIRE IMMORTELLE D'ASSURER L'INDEPENDANCE DES ETATS-UNIS D'AMERIQUE.

REQUIESCAT IN PACE.

CETTE PLAQUE COMMEMORATIVE A ETE PLACEE PAR LES SOINS DE LA SOCIETE
DES CINCINNATI DE FRANCE, LE 19 OCTOBRE 1931, CENT-CINQUANTIEME
ANNIVERSAIRE DE LA CAPITULATION DE YORKTOWN ET EN SOUVENIR DE CE
FAIT D'ARMES DONT LES CONSEQUENCES SONT INCALCULABLES.

(back of the church, behind the altar)

It was the British, however, who arrived first at the Chesapeake; but, not finding de Grasse, went to look for him in New York. De Grasse calmly entered the Chesapeake a few days later on August 28 and began to disembark the reinforcements that La Fayette was waiting for at Williamsburg.

In the meantime, Admiral Hood, not finding de Grasse in New York, sailed rapidly down the coast again with Admiral Graves, commander of the New York fleet. On September 5, they appeared at the entrance to the Chesapeake with fourteen ships-of-the-line while de Grasse was still unloading his men. Fortunately, the courteous British, lined up in battle formation off the Chesapeake Capes, waited until de Grasse had hastily reached open water before engaging in combat.

The British fleet was no match for de Grasse's twenty-four ships carrying 1700 guns and 19,000 seamen! After a two-hour battle, the French won the day. Both fleets then spent the next few days manoeuvering on the open sea without fighting. This allowed Admiral de Barras to slip in unnoticed to the Chesapeake to deliver the heavy artillery from Newport and ferry Rochambeau's and Washington's soldiers from Annapolis to Williamsburg!

When Washington arrived on September 14, he was overjoyed to find de Grasse waiting unopposed at the entrance to the Chesapeake. The British fleet had limped back to New York for repairs and had left Cornwallis in the lurch. De Grasse assured Washington that he would remain until the allied troops could force Cornwallis' surrender.

And so he did. His powerful fleet blocked the Chesapeake and prevented all help from reaching Cornwallis while French and American forces on land blockaded him in Yorktown. Thanks to de Grasse, the allies won the Battle of Yorktown and American independence became a reality.

After the victory on October 19th, all the leaders boarded the "Ville de Paris" to celebrate with de Grasse. Washington, Rochambeau, and La Fayette were there. De Grasse, a giant almost as tall as Washington, amused everyone by calling him "mon petit Général"! De Grasse, himself, never set foot on American soil.

De Grasse's final years were undeservedly difficult. Returning to patrol the West Indies, he lost a battle to the British Admiral Rodney in April 1782. He was taken prisoner to London where he was treated, nonetheless, with respect. On his return to France, he was court-martialed, but found not guilty. De Grasse died in Paris in January 1788.

The sadness of those final years was lightened, however, by Washington's continued support and praise, his nomination as a founding member of the Cincinnati Society, and a gift from Congress of four cannons captured at Yorktown. They stand proudly at the gate of his Château at Tilly, in witness to the enduring gratitude of the American people.

A statue depicting de Grasse on the bridge of the "Ville de Paris" stands on avenue des Nations-Unies, opposite rue Le Nôtre, Paris 16e. The monument was inaugurated in 1931 to commemorate the 150th anniversary of Yorktown.

SQUARE YORKTOWN

Victory for the Americans
Paris 16e
METRO: Trocadéro

This small square off the southwest corner of Place du Trocadéro celebrates the great victory which made the independence of the United States possible and forced the British to give up their thirteen colonies in America.

The victory at Yorktown was the culmination of a six-year struggle that the colonies, at times, seemed to have little chance of winning. As Washington's and Rochambeau's troops converged on La Fayette's and the Marquis de Saint Simon's forces at Williamsburg in mid-September 1781, little did they realize that victory was, at last, at hand.

Reassured that de Grasse's fleet was blocking the entrance to the Chesapeake and preventing help from reaching Cornwallis who was solidly entrenched at Yorktown, Washington gave the order to march from Williamsburg. On September 28, the combined forces of nearly 16,000 men marched unopposed and set up camp within a mile of the town.

With Cornwallis trapped in Yorktown, the allies' objective was to besiege the town until the British surrendered. The allied forces occupied a line that extended in a great curve for some six miles around the town. Rochambeau and Saint Simon spread out on the left flank with 7500 men, while 8000 American militia and Continentals took the right flank. La Fayette commanded his elite troops of Light Cavalry.

On August 30, realizing how precarious his situation was, Cornwallis abandoned his outer defenses except for a couple of redoubts. This allowed Washington to move his artillery to within 1000 yards of the British lines.

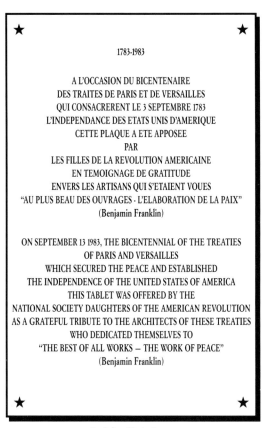

1783-1983

A L'OCCASION DU BICENTENAIRE
DES TRAITES DE PARIS ET DE VERSAILLES
QUI CONSACRERENT LE 3 SEPTEMBRE 1783
L'INDEPENDANCE DES ETATS UNIS D'AMERIQUE
CETTE PLAQUE A ETE APPOSEE
PAR
LES FILLES DE LA REVOLUTION AMERICAINE
EN TEMOIGNAGE DE GRATITUDE
ENVERS LES ARTISANS QUI S'ETAIENT VOUES
"AU PLUS BEAU DES OUVRAGES · L'ELABORATION DE LA PAIX"
(Benjamin Franklin)

ON SEPTEMBER 13 1983, THE BICENTENNIAL OF THE TREATIES
OF PARIS AND VERSAILLES
WHICH SECURED THE PEACE AND ESTABLISHED
THE INDEPENDENCE OF THE UNITED STATES OF AMERICA
THIS TABLET WAS OFFERED BY THE
NATIONAL SOCIETY DAUGHTERS OF THE AMERICAN REVOLUTION
AS A GRATEFUL TRIBUTE TO THE ARCHITECTS OF THESE TREATIES
WHO DEDICATED THEMSELVES TO
"THE BEST OF ALL WORKS – THE WORK OF PEACE"
(Benjamin Franklin)

Look for tablet in the grass

The real work of the siege could then begin. Large-scale siege warfare was something new to Washington's army, and the skilled French engineers and artillery men proved to be invaluable advisors. Under their supervision, on the night of October 6, the first line of siege was begun. The British awoke to find a trench 2000 yards long that had been dug by 1500 men during the night!

Two days later, the heavy artillery opened fire on the British positions. General Washington, himself, fired the first round from the American side. Despondent, Cornwallis watched while his defenses crumbled under the fire of Colonel d'Aboville using the new French Gribeauval cannons—a fire he had never before encountered!

The bombardment was so effective that the allies began work on their second parallel siege line. On the 14th, two detachments, one French under Count Guillaume des Deux-Ponts, and one American under Colonel Alexander Hamilton, stormed the two remaining British redoubts. The relentless bombardments continued.

Finally, on the morning of October 17, a red-coated drummer boy appeared on the British rampart with an officer holding a white handkerchief. The allied guns fell silent. A victory had been won!

Washington insisted on unconditional surrender which Cornwallis signed on October 19th. That same afternoon, 7000 British troops, led by General O'Hara, marched out of Yorktown between two parallel lines of French and American soldiers and officers. The French, dressed in white uniforms and flying a white silk flag embroidered with golden *fleurs-de-lys*, faced the Americans whose faces bespoke the hardships and privations that they had endured in the long struggle for freedom. As the fifes and drums played "The World Turned Upside Down," General O'Hara, representing Cornwallis, who pleaded illness, rode over to Rochambeau to present his sword. Rochambeau's aide-de-camp, gesturing to Washington astride his horse, said simply, "Our Commander-in-Chief, Sir, is General Washington."

Although peace would not be signed in Paris until September 1783, nearly two years later, Yorktown marked the decisive victory of the War of Independence.

The Duke of Lauzun sailed immediately to bring the good news to Versailles. Louis XVI asked every bishop in France to celebrate a *Te Deum* in thanksgiving for the victory at Yorktown.

BENJAMIN FRANKLIN
1706–1790

LE GENIE QUI AFFRANCHIT
L'AMERIQUE ET VERSA SUR
L'EUROPE DES TORRENTS DE
LUMIERE : LE SAGE QUE
DEUX MONDES RECLAMENT

On the square stands a statue of Benjamin Franklin offered to the city of Paris by John H. Harpes. It is the work of J. J. Boyle. The bas-reliefs by F. Brou show Franklin being presented to the Court of Louis XVI at Versailles and the signing of the Treaty of Paris in 1783.

To the left of the statue of Franklin is a monument built in 1931 that lists all the French soldiers and officers who died at Yorktown. In all, some 2,500 Frenchmen gave their lives in the War of Independence.

8

PLACE DES ETATS-UNIS

**Statue of Washington and La Fayette
Paris 16e
METRO: Iéna, Kléber, or Boissière**

This quiet tree-lined square and garden as well as its neighboring "quartier" are full of mementos of the Franco-American alliance in the War of Independence.

The square was created in 1866 and named Place des Etats-Unis in 1881 when the U.S. legation office was transferred here. At the west end stands a monument honoring Washington and La Fayette. The bronze statues were sculpted by Bartholdi, who also created the Statue of Liberty, and donated by Joseph Pulitzer who presented them to the city of Paris on July 4, 1895. The inauguration ceremony featured John Philip Souza and his sixty-piece band.

There are other American mementos on the square from other times. President Woodrow Wilson resided at number 11 in 1919 when he attended the Peace Conference. At the east end of the Place is a monument to the American volunteers in World War I who joined the French Army before the U.S. went to war in 1917, the way La Fayette, La Rouerie, Du Portail, Mauduit, and L'Enfant had done before 1778!

Place des Etats-Unis is surrounded by streets and monuments honoring heroes of the War of Independence:

- Place de l'Amiral de Grasse at the east end of the square commemorates the Admiral's role in the victory at Yorktown.

- Rue la Pérouse, at the northwest corner of the square, is named for the commander of the "l'Amazone," one of the ships that took Rochambeau's army to the New World. During the War, La Pérouse sailed back and forth carrying messages between France and Europe.

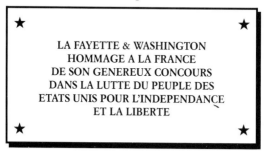

★   ★

LA FAYETTE & WASHINGTON
HOMMAGE A LA FRANCE
DE SON GENEREUX CONCOURS
DANS LA LUTTE DU PEUPLE DES
ETATS UNIS POUR L'INDEPENDANCE
ET LA LIBERTE

★   ★

- Rue de l'Amiral d'Estaing, going south from the western end of Place des Etats-Unis, is named for Admiral Charles Henri, Comte d'Estaing, who commanded the first fleet sent to America to help the Insurgents. Although he won a major victory off Grenada in 1779, his attempts to dislodge the British from Newport in 1778 and Savannah in 1779 were both unsuccessful. Georgia made him an honorary citizen in 1785.

- Place d'Iéna, one block south of the Place on Avenue d'Iéna. Here stands the statue of George Washington, the work of Daniel Chester French. It was offered by the Women of the United States of America.

- Place Rochambeau, one block southeast of the Place via rue Freycinet. Statue of Rochambeau by F. Hamar.

9

HOTEL D'YORK

Treaty of Paris. Independence recognized by England
56, rue Jacob, Paris 6e
METRO: Saint-Germain-des-Prés

In this building, on September 3, 1783, the representatives of the United States and the king of England signed the Treaty of Paris by which England recognized the independence of the thirteen colonies. The most important sentence of the treaty read: "His Britannic Majesty acknowledges the United States of America to be free, sovereign and independent." America's existence as a sovereign state was at last a reality, and there was no one to challenge it!

David Hartley and Richard Oswald signed the treaty on behalf of England. The United States was represented by three giants of American history: Benjamin Franklin, John Jay, and John Adams. Jay was to become the first Chief Justice in 1789. Adams, after serving as the first U.S. Ambassador to the Court of St. James, would serve two terms as Vice-President under George Washington before being elected the second President of the United States in 1797. Franklin would stay on as the first U.S. Ambassador to the Court of Versailles until 1785. The treaty was ratified early in 1784 by the U.S. Congress assembled in Annapolis.

That eventful day, the ever-courteous British had brought a gift from George III for each of the American negotiators. The customary present—the royal portrait framed in diamonds—would have certainly offended the Americans, so each was given 1000 pounds instead! The British were becoming fast learners in New World psychology!

A lot had changed since 1778 when France had first recognized American independence and sent troops and warships to help the Insurgents. France had found herself at war on several fronts with England as hostilities spread from the former colonies to the West Indies and Gibraltar. Spain, who had interests in the New World as well, was only a lukewarm ally.

EN CE BATIMENT
JADIS HOTEL D'YORK
LE 5 SEPTEMBRE 1783

DAVID HARTLEY,
AU NOM DU ROI D'ANGLETERRE
BENJAMIN FRANKLIN,
JOHN JAY, JOHN ADAMS
AU NOM DES ETATS-UNIS D'AMERIQUE
ONT SIGNE LE TRAITE DEFINITIF DE PAIX
RECONNAISSANT L'INDEPENDANCE
DES ETATS-UNIS

The battle of Yorktown in October 1781 had been the decisive victory in the American War of Independence, but hostilities between France and England dragged on for nearly two more years. British Admiral Rodney defeated de Grasse in the West Indies in April 1782 and took him prisoner to London. The combined efforts of France and Spain couldn't rout the British from Gibraltar.

As the war spluttered along, the three American peace commissioners, Jay, Adams and Franklin, began to negotiate a "preliminary" separate peace with the British which was signed in November 1782. Congress and the U.S. Minister of Foreign Affairs, Robert Livingston, were furious to see their orders of "no separate peace" violated. The French considered it—and still do—very bad manners. But the Americans saw in it the recognition of their independence, and that is what counts! The French Foreign Minister, Vergennes, still convinced the King to lend more money to the new country: 6,000,000 pounds at 5%. But all is well that ends well. The official treaty in 1783 ended the war between the "mother country" and her former colonies.

That same day, in Versailles, official peace treaties were signed between England and France and England and Spain, and celebrated with a gala dinner for all.

That night, John Jay wrote in his diary: "If we are not happy today, we will never be happy!"

The building and the room on the second floor where the treaty was signed cannot be visited. A plaque on the left side of the building recalls the historic event that took place here.

From 1762 to 1768, a poor but brilliant mathematics student, Jean-Antoine Nicolas Caritat, Marquis de Condorcet, lived on the top floor of this building. He was a friend of Jefferson's. (chapter 17 page 69).

10

HOTEL DE VALENTINOIS

Benjamin Franklin's Residence: 1777 - 1785
Corner of rue Raynouard and rue Singer, Paris 16e
MÉTRO: Passy or Muette

This was the site of Franklin's home for nearly ten years. Today, only a very tall plaque and a portrait of Franklin on a modern building at the corner of rue Raynouard and rue Singer recall Franklin's stay in Passy. In the eighteenth century, Passy was a village outside Paris. American diplomats tended to gravitate here or to nearby Auteuil. Whether they were following Franklin or looking for less expensive lodgings, they were called "the Gentlemen from Passy." In any case, it was a good location for diplomats: a little bit away from Paris on the way to Versailles!

When the seventy-one-year-old Franklin arrived in Paris in 1777, he was invited to stay with Le Ray de Chaumont, an international merchant who had made a fortune trading with East India and who was supplying the Insurgents with gunpowder. He owned the sumptuous Hôtel de Valentinois (some called it a château) in Passy with an eighteen-acre garden overlooking Paris and the river Seine. He did not accept rent from Franklin who first settled in an independent pavilion called the "Basse Cour."

It was here that Franklin lived and worked with the other members of the American mission to the Court of France, Arthur Lee, Silas Deane and later John

---

45

Adams and John Jay. It was here, too, that Franklin conducted experiments on electricity, and, in another building, set up a printing press. Towards the end of his stay, Franklin moved into the main house. After he was officially named Ambassador to France, he insisted on paying rent to Chaumont.

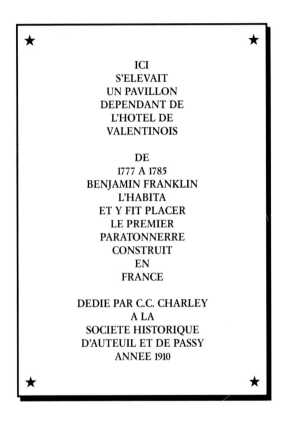

ICI
S'ELEVAIT
UN PAVILLON
DEPENDANT DE
L'HOTEL DE
VALENTINOIS

DE
1777 A 1785
BENJAMIN FRANKLIN
L'HABITA
ET Y FIT PLACER
LE PREMIER
PARATONNERRE
CONSTRUIT
EN
FRANCE

DEDIE PAR C.C. CHARLEY
A LA
SOCIETE HISTORIQUE
D'AUTEUIL ET DE PASSY
ANNEE 1910

To the north, rue Raynouard leads to rue Franklin, named after him in 1791. It ends at Square Yorktown with his statue (chapter 7 page 39).

Franklin was enormously popular all through his stay. He was already well known in Paris from his previous visits in 1767 and 1769. He had many contacts with the French intelligentsia especially the Physiocrats and Masons. He had received personal congratulations for his experiments on electricity from King

Louis XV. When he rode from Nantes to Paris in 1776, crowds lined the roads to acclaim him! John Adams was so amazed by France's admiration for him that he wrote: "When they spoke of him, they seemed to think that he was to restore the golden age!"

Not only the ladies at Versailles but all Frenchmen were impressed by his intelligence and scientific knowledge. The most brilliant minds came to Passy to visit him: Turgot, Buffon, d'Alembert, Condorcet, La Rouchefoucauld, Malesherbes, Raynal, Beaumarchais, Mirabeau,...He was received by the King at Versailles. The Masonic Lodge of the Nine Sisters, where he escorted Voltaire shortly before he died, made him Grand Master. The Académie des Sciences, where he had been elected in 1772, convened a special meeting for Voltaire and Franklin together; and when they embraced, everyone said it was Solon embracing Sophocles![1]

On November 20, 1783, Franklin witnessed the first balloon ascension with the Marquis d'Arlande[2] and Pilâtre de Rozier. As the crowd cheered, the two aeronauts lifted off from the Château de la Muette in Passy. Franklin was asked to sign the official report of the event along with representatives of the King and of the Academy of Sciences. When somebody said: "Of what use is this new invention?" Franklin replied: "Of what use is a new-born child?"

Without hesitation, it can be said that it was Franklin's prestige and brilliant diplomatic skills that convinced the French to help the Insurgents. Thanks to him, France provided arms, ammunition and troops, but also the diplomatic recognition that helped the Americans win their freedom from Great Britain.

Franklin went back to America in 1785. During a long and brilliant career in the service of his country, he was the signer of four of the major documents giving birth to the United States; the Declaration of Independence (1776), the Treaty with France (1778), the Treaty of Paris with England (1783), and the U.S. Constitution (1787).

When the news of his death reached Paris in 1790, the

emotion was such that, in the middle of the French Revolution, the National Assembly decided to adjourn for the day. The following year, rue Franklin was named for him. Today, the street plaque reads rue Benjamin Franklin 1706–1790, Physicist and American Statesman. The great Jefferson said that succeeding Franklin as Ambassador to France was a lesson in humility!

Franklin was never forgotten. When the violent and anti-religious French Assembly, La Convention, changed the calendar in 1793, it replaced Christian saints by Republican heroes. Benjamin Franklin was one of them; his day was June 12th. The calendar remained in use until 1805.

[1] Solon: *Greek lawmaker (640–558 B.C.). Gave Athens a more democratic constitution, boosted the Athenians' national pride and lowered taxes on the poor.*

Sophocles: *Greek dramatist (495–405) B.C.) Author of Antigone, Electra, Oedipus-Rex, Ajax,…*

[2] *Two brothers of the Marquis d'Arlande had fought with the army of Rochambeau in America.*

11

HOTEL ANTIER

John Adams' Residence, 1784 - 1785
also called Hôtel des Demoiselles de Verrières
43-47, rue d'Auteuil, Paris 16e
METRO: Michel Ange-Auteuil

John Adams, who later became the second President of the United States, resided here with his wife, Abigail and his two grown children Nabby and John Quincy, who was elected the sixth president of the United States in 1825. The family lived here in Auteuil for almost a year between September 1784 and August 1785.

John Adams had first come to Paris in April 1778 with his son John Quincy who was only ten years old. To while away the long hours of the ocean trip, he dutifully studied French, but without much success. Fear of being captured by the British and taken prisoner to England was a constant distraction.

Once in Paris, Adams replaced Silas Deane on the commission with Franklin to negotiate help for the United States under the Treaties of Friendship and Commerce which had been signed that February. However, he did not get along with Franklin who was always dining with fancy ladies and brilliant philosophers. In September, Congress decided to appoint Franklin sole Minister Plenipotentiary to the Court of France, and Adams returned home.

In February 1780, he was back once again to work with Franklin and John Jay who were trying to negotiate a treaty of peace and commerce with England. At this time, the agenda was war, not peace, and Adams had nothing to do. He spent his time preaching morality to anyone he could talk to, including Vergennes, the French Foreign Minister who got tired of him.

Congress found him a job and sent him to Amsterdam as Minister Plenipotentiary to negotiate a loan from

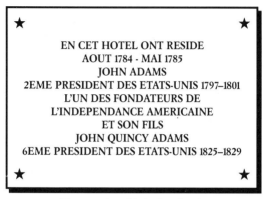

EN CET HOTEL ONT RESIDE
AOUT 1784 - MAI 1785
JOHN ADAMS
2EME PRESIDENT DES ETATS-UNIS 1797–1801
L'UN DES FONDATEURS DE
L'INDEPENDANCE AMERICAINE
ET SON FILS
JOHN QUINCY ADAMS
6EME PRESIDENT DES ETATS-UNIS 1825–1829

(Plaque on the wall behind small garden)

the Dutch. For two years, he shuttled back and forth between Paris and Amsterdam where his real business was. His efforts were finally rewarded when the Netherlands recognized the United States on April 1782 and signed a treaty of commerce in October.

While still Minister Plenipotentiary, he worked with Jay and Franklin to negotiate a "preliminary separate peace" with the British which was signed in November 1782.

It was in the summer of 1784 that Abigail and the children came to Paris to join him, and the family settled in Auteuil.

John Adams is probably the earliest Ugly American. He hardly enjoyed France or Paris. He resented the luxury in which people lived and was shocked that Franklin lived like a French aristocrat! In his own words: "The life of Doctor Franklin was a scene of continual dissipation." He did not appreciate having to pay customs duties for the twenty-five bottles of wine he had brought from Bordeaux. He resented the craze about Parisian fashion and considered it a tax levied by the French on the world! He resented French servants with their set tasks. His distrust of the French only intensified after attending a performance of Beaumarchais' *Marriage of Figaro* at the Comédie Française. He viewed it as a piece of "studied deception and intrigue."

He was shocked by the sight of Franklin embracing Voltaire in front of the Academy of Sciences. Moreover, Abigail was shocked by the indecent dresses of French actresses and by the "négligés" of Madame Helvetius.

There were, however, a few things that he did enjoy in Paris: a flight in the Montgolfier brothers' balloon and the public baths at the Pont Royal which provided hot towels! But all the while, he longed for his home and farm in Quincy, Massachusetts.

In the spring of 1785, John Adams was happy to be appointed the first American Ambassador to the Court of Saint James, and he left Paris and his lovely garden on the rue d'Auteuil. Only Abigail, however, was sad to leave.

George III welcomed him with these "warm" remarks: "As I have been the last person in the kingdom to recognize America's independence; now that it is established, I wish to be the last one in my kingdom to violate it."

From London, Adams wrote to Jefferson who was selecting, buying and shipping him the best wines in France: "Stop the shipments or I will be ruined!" He had just discovered that, as ambassador, he was allowed only 500 duty-free bottles of wine. Over that amount, he would have to pay $1.75 per bottle to his gracious Majesty's customs.

Still longing for his home in Quincy, Adams asked to return to the United States in 1788.

Adams also visited his famous neighbor, Madame Helvetius at 59, rue d'Auteuil. The widow of the famous philosopher, Helvetius, she was, herself, an eccentric, but also one of the most brilliant minds of the century. She welcomed the Paris intelligentsia to her home. Franklin adored her, visited her every Saturday for dinner, and, according to some, proposed to her!

One of the guests of "Our Lady of Auteuil," as she was called, was Father (Abbé) Morellet, a member of the French Academy and a fan of the Insurgents. At the end of a merry dinner, he wrote a song which begins:

> On ne combattit jamais
> Pour de plus grand intérêts:
> Ils veulent l'indépendance
> Pour boire des vins de France.
> C'est là le fin
> Du projet de Benjamin.

and translates as follows:

> One does not fight
> For a better cause:
> They want their independence
> To drink the wines of France.
> That is the goal
> Of Benjamin's plan.

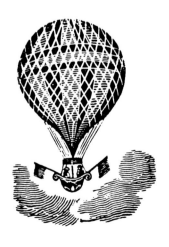

12

HOTEL DE LANGEAC

Thomas Jefferson's residence: 1785 - 1789
92, avenue des Champs-Elysées, Paris 8e
Metro: George V

This is the site of the former Hôtel de Langeac.
Thomas Jefferson moved here when he was officially
appointed Ambassador to France in 1785. At the time,
he had already been in Paris for a year working with
Franklin, who had then returned home, and with
Adams, who was newly appointed Ambassador to
Great Britain. Brand new at the time, the Hôtel de
Langeac, built by the architect Chalgrin, was located
just within the city limits. The building at 92, avenue
des Champs-Elysées which replaces the spacious
mansion and its large garden bears a plaque donated
by the students of the University of Virginia who
served in France in World War I. Inside the building, there is another memento with the portrait of
Jefferson. It reads: "Ici vécut Thomas Jefferson
(1743 - 1826), Troisième Président des Etats-Unis,
Ambassadeur des Etats-Unis en France de 1785 à
1789."

Jefferson lived here with William Short, his chargé
d'affaires, and his black servant, James Hemings,
whom he sent to learn French cooking with a Parisian
caterer. His maître d'hôtel, valet de chambre, a coach-
man, gardener and cook completed the household.
Jefferson's two daughters, Patsy and Mary, joined him
the same year. Patsy, whom her friends called "Jeff,"

attended boarding school at the Abbaye Royale de Pentemont across the river. Her younger sister Mary enrolled in 1787. Jefferson enjoyed the large garden and used it to grow what he could not find in Paris, especially sweet corn. He ordered corn, sweet potato, and watermelon seeds from North Carolina!

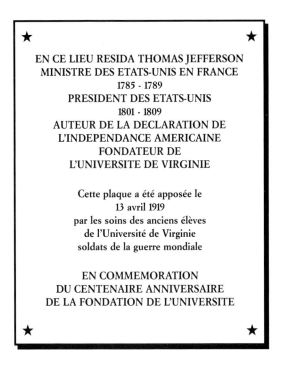

EN CE LIEU RESIDA THOMAS JEFFERSON
MINISTRE DES ETATS-UNIS EN FRANCE
1785 - 1789
PRESIDENT DES ETATS-UNIS
1801 - 1809
AUTEUR DE LA DECLARATION DE
L'INDEPENDANCE AMERICAINE
FONDATEUR DE
L'UNIVERSITE DE VIRGINIE

Cette plaque a été apposée le
13 avril 1919
par les soins des anciens élèves
de l'Université de Virginie
soldats de la guerre mondiale

EN COMMEMORATION
DU CENTENAIRE ANNIVERSAIRE
DE LA FONDATION DE L'UNIVERSITE

When Jefferson went to Versailles to present his credentials to the King, Louis XVI said: "So, you are the man who replaces Doctor Franklin?" "No, your Majesty," replied Jefferson, "nobody can replace Doctor Franklin. I am only his successor!" Jefferson's primary task as Ambassador was to enforce the terms of the Treaty of Paris which put an end to the War of Independence and to facilitate trade relations between France and the United States.

Jefferson, who had been the inspiration of the new Republic, arrived in France when it was still an absolute monarchy, and witnessed the beginning of the

French Revolution. His prestige was such that he was invited to sit in on the National Assembly committee which was drafting a constitution. He did not accept, but the leaders of the patriots' party met at his home many times to ask his advice. Each time, Jefferson sent a note to the Minister of Foreign Affairs, informing him of the meeting. Jefferson did, however, draft certain technical documents for the French. When La Fayette sat at his desk to draft the French Declaration of the Rights of Man, he pinned a copy of Jefferson's Declaration of Independence to the wall in front of him to give him inspiration.

During his stay in Paris, Jefferson enjoyed walking around the city for long hours. He visited the Jardin des Plantes and its director, Buffon, whose works he greatly respected. He purchased furniture, prints and engravings that he later took back to Monticello.

Jefferson had two great passions: books and wine. He purchased many books in Paris that he eventually brought back to Monticello (chapter 16 page 65).

Jefferson's knowledge of wine is quite exceptional for his time, especially for an American. He studied how vines were planted, grown, and pruned; how they were selected and used; how wine was made, measured and sold. He made his first observations in the vineyards at Suresnes, just outside Paris, but he also travelled to many wine-growing areas: the Rhine Valley, Champagne, Burgundy, the Rhône Valley, Italy, Languedoc, Bordeaux and the Loire Valley.

Jefferson knew how to describe a wine. He used the terms light, color, strength, weakness, astringent, rough, acid...and differentiated between silky and sweet.

He also knew how to buy wine for himself, for the first U.S. Ambassador to London, John Adams, and for the first President at the White House, George Washington. His motto was simple: "Quality first, then price"!

He learned the importance of vintage years, the different growths and producers. He discovered that it was better to buy from growers than from dealers. At a time when there were no regulations, no guidebooks, and no wine magazines, he selected Yquem, Laffite, Haut Brion, LaTour, and Château Margaux from Bordeaux, and Chambertin, Vougeot, and Montrachet from Burgundy. His favorite wine was Meursault Goutte d'Or 1784 from Monsieur Bachey.

Jefferson ordered silver cups from the silversmith Odiot. The House of Odiot, founded in 1690, is still in business and sells "Jefferson cups." It is located at 7, place de la Madeleine and is open every day from 9:30 a.m. to 6:30 p.m.

13

RUE DE RICHELIEU

Residence of four American Presidents
Paris 2e
METRO: Bourse or Palais Royal

Almost one kilometer long, rue de Richelieu is a non-descript narrow street running from the Boulevard des Italiens to the Comédie Française and the Guichets du Louvre on the rue de Rivoli. Going south on this one-way street, one notices only the quiet Square Louvois facing the entrance to the Bibliothèque Nationale and the long, imposing library building, itself, between the rue Colbert and the rue des Petits-Champs. Formerly the Royal Library founded six centuries ago, the Bibliothèque Nationale is the equivalent of the Library of Congress, today.

It is hard to imagine that the rue de Richelieu was a very busy and elegant street in the eighteenth century. At the time of the American Revolution, many gracious seventeenth-century mansions had been converted into chic hotels. That is the reason why so many American visitors stayed here.

Walking north from the rue de Rivoli, one can discover:

No. 17: John Adams stayed briefly at the Hôtel de Valois on his arrival from Bordeaux in April 1778, and again, in October 1782, when he came to sign the "preliminaries of peace." He later moved to Auteuil. The original building no longer exists.

No. 30: Thomas Jefferson stayed at the Hôtel d'Orléans after his arrival in August 1784. He then moved to another hotel on what is now rue Bonaparte, before settling at the corner of rue de Berri and the Champs-Elysées. (chapter 12 page 53) The original building still stands.

No. 95: James Monroe stayed here after his arrival in Le Havre in July 1794. He came to replace Ambassador Gouverneur Morris. Robespierre had just been guillotined, and the Reign of Terror had finally ended. One of Monroe's first duties was to see that Thomas Paine was set free from prison (chapter 21 page 80). Sick and penniless after his ordeal, Paine stayed here while Monroe cared for him. It was here that he finished writing *The Age of Reason.* Formerly the Hôtel des Patriotes Etrangers, it is now the Hôtel Cusset.

No. 97: John Quincy Adams, who was to become the sixth U.S. President, stayed at the Hôtel du Nord from February to May 1815. The hotel later became the Hôtel des Princes and was partially taken down to open the Passage des Princes. After having lived in Paris with his parents in the 1780's, Adams returned in 1815 while he was U.S. Ambassador to London. At the time, Louis XVI's brother, Louis XVIII, had been called to be king of France after Napoléon's defeat and exile. Adams witnessed Napoléon's return to Paris after his escape from Elba in what was known as the "Hundred Days."

Several other participants in America's Independence have a connection with the rue de Richelieu:

- Gouverneur Morris, Jefferson's successor as Ambassador to Paris, lived at the Hôtel Richelieu for two years, at number 63, rue de Richelieu. It is now the Grand Hôtel de Malte.

- The Duc de Lauzun, who led the French cavalry at Yorktown, was born on this street.

  From rue de Richelieu, one can easily walk to the gardens of the Palais Royal. One of the liveliest meeting-places in Paris at the time of Franklin, John Paul Jones, and Jefferson, it was well known for its restaurants, bars, cafes, gambling and ladies. Today, one can still admire the elegant eighteenth-century facades overlooking the gardens and browse in the quiet shopping arcade.

Enter the Palais Royal gardens from either end of the rue Montpensier, which runs parallel to rue de Richelieu, or through the passageway at 24, rue Montpensier.

To reach rue de Montpensier from rue de Richelieu, use one of the quaint passageways at 26, 34 or 52, rue de Richelieu.

LA BOURSE DE COMMERCE

La Halle aux Blés
1, rue de Viarmes, Paris ler
MÉTRO: Les Halles

The Bourse de Commerce is the former Halle aux Blés or municipal grain market built for the City of Paris between 1763 and 1766 by Camus de Mézières. Grain storage was most important at a time when a poor wheat crop could start a revolt if not a revolution.

In 1782, the rotunda was covered with a wooden cupola by the architects J.G. Legrand and Jacques Molinos. Using a technique suggested by the Renaissance architect, Philibert de L'Orme, two hundred years earlier, they inserted twenty-five windows between the wooden ribs of the structure. Bright daylight flooded the interior of the market. The innovative concept and attractive proportions of the rotunda made it one of the main attractions in Paris.

In 1783, La Halle aux Blés was the scene of a festival celebrating the signing of the Treaty of Paris. On December 14th, 6000 people crowded into the rotunda and danced to the tunes of an orchestra. Bread, wine, and sausage were on the house! That evening, the interior was lit by 6000 candles.

In July 1790, after the news of Benjamin Franklin's death had reached Paris and the National Assembly had listened to Mirabeau's eulogy and voted three days of national mourning, the city of Paris decided to have its own ceremony. It took place on July 21st in the Rotunda, as the Halle aux Blés was called. A bust of Franklin was placed in the center of the black-draped building, and Abbé Fauchet gave a funeral oration in front of the Mayor, a delegation from the National Assembly, and 4000 Parisians.

The Halle aux Blés, however, has the strongest ties to Jefferson. It was here that on a lovely day in August 1786, he met Maria Cosway. He was introduced to her by the painter, John Trumbull, who had been a classmate of her brother, George Hadfield. Some say that the encounter took place at the foot of the Medicis Column which still stands on one side of the building today. In the 1570's, Catherine de Medicis used to climb its 147 stairs with her Florentine astrologer, Ruggieri, who predicted that her three sons would become kings of France.

That day, Jefferson cancelled his dinner engagement with the old Duchesse de La Rochefoucauld in order to enjoy Maria's company. He took the Cosways on many sight-seeing expeditions during their stay in Paris: Reuilly, Marly, Saint-Germain, Louveciennes,...

When they left Paris, Jefferson wrote Maria that famous twelve-page letter, the dialogue between his Head and his Heart which now rests in the Library of Congress in Washington. Although he had told her to read only one or two pages a day, she read the whole letter right away and discovered that the Heart had the last word.

Perhaps because of this romantic episode, Jefferson became enamored with the architecture of the Halle aux Blés. Not only did he start building a skyroom under a dome at Monticello, but he suggested the Philibert de l'Orme dome for many public buildings in the United States: a market in Richmond, the White House, a dry dock in Washington, the House of Representatives...all to no avail! Jefferson finally won his point for the Monumental Church in Richmond which still stands today with a wooden dome à la Philibert de l'Orme!

The dome that Jefferson never forgot burned in 1802 and was rebuilt with an iron frame. The building was further modified in the late nineteenth century with the addition of a baroque facade which hides the soft lines of the dome. However, in this building which is, today, a commodity exchange and a business center run by the Paris Chamber of Commerce, one can still climb up and down the double spiral staircase that Jefferson climbed, stand in the middle of the rotunda where Benjamin Franklin's bust stood in 1790 and look outside at the foot of the Medicis tower where Jefferson saw Maria Cosway's curly golden hair in the August light!

Open 8 a.m. to 7 p.m.
(Monday then Friday)
Tel 01.55.65.55.65.

15

CAFE PROCOPE

**Patronized by Benjamin Franklin,
Thomas Jefferson, John Paul Jones, Voltaire
13, rue de l'Ancienne Comédie, Paris 6e
METRO: Odéon**

A plaque to the left side of the main entrance tells us that the Procope was established in 1686 by a Sicilian Francesco Procopio. It is the oldest café in Paris and the first place where coffee was served to the public. Although the café has been recently restored, the building has changed little since the seventeenth century. The café, which is also a restaurant, has been a popular meeting-place over the centuries for writers, philosophers, revolutionaries...and many famous Americans. We know for sure that the Procope was patronized by John Paul Jones, Thomas Jefferson and Benjamin Franklin, who is still remembered on the menu today by a "Coupe Benjamin Franklin."

When the Comédie Française opened just across the street at number 14 in 1689, the café attracted writers and theater-goers. After the theater moved to new quarters in 1770, philosophers and revolutionaries took their place...Voltaire, Rousseau, Beaumarchais, Danton, Robespierre. Voltaire's desk can be seen on the second floor. Young Lieutenant Bonaparte left his hat in hock there...as the story goes.

On June 15, 1790, after the National Assembly had adjourned to mourn Benjamin Franklin's death, the

CAFE PROCOPE

ICI
PROCOPIO DEI COLTELLI
FONDA EN 1686
LE TRES ANCIEN CAFE PROCOPE
ET LE PLUS CELEBRE CENTRE
DE LA VIE LITTERAIRE ET PHILOSOPHIQUE
AU 18e et au 19e SIECLES.
IL FUT FREQUENTE PAR
LA FONTAINE, VOLTAIRE,
LES ENCYCLOPEDISTES,
BENJAMIN FRANKLIN, DANTON, MARAT,
ROBESPIERRE, NAPOLEON BONAPARTE,
BALZAC, VICTOR HUGO,
GAMBETTA, VERLAINE
ET ANATOLE FRANCE.

"True Friends of Liberty" met at the Procope. Monsieur de la Fite, a lawyer, held a memorial service in front of Franklin's portrait.

Open from 9 a.m. to 12 p.m. (all year)

IN THE STEPS OF THOMAS JEFFERSON

Beginnings of the Library of Congress
Quai des Grands Augustins, Paris 6e
METRO: Saint-Michel

Walking along the River Seine on the Quai des Grands Augustins, one will immediately notice book stalls ("les bouquinistes") on the river parapet and book shops on the other side of the street. The bookstores were already there in Jefferson's time. The left bank had been the center of the book trade for centuries.

Jefferson loved to walk along the river almost daily looking for books. During his five years in Paris, he nearly doubled the size of his personal library which he had begun as a young man in Virginia.

In a letter to Samuel Harrison Smith, Jefferson wrote: "While residing in Paris, I devoted every afternoon I was disengaged, for a summer or two, in examining all the principal bookstores, turning over every book with my own hands, and putting by everything related to America, and indeed what was rare and valuable in every science."

Among Jefferson's best suppliers was J.-F. Froullé, both a bookseller and publisher at 35, quai des Grands Augustins. This is how Jefferson recommended him to James Monroe: "I can assure you, that, having run a severe gauntlet under the Paris book-sellers, I rested at last on this old gentleman, whom I found, in a long and intimate course of dealings, to be one of the most conscientiously honest men I ever had dealings with. I recommend him to you strongly, should you purchase books."

Apparently, Jefferson did not mind that Froullé made out his invoices to "Monsieur Chefersone."

In 1788, Froullé published a translation from the Italian of Mazzei's book, *Recherches Historiques et Politiques sur les Etats-Unis*...page 67. This book included "Four Letters from a Burgher in New Haven," written by Condorcet (chapter 17 page 70) who, together with his wife, supervised the translation of Mazzei's book.

At 21, quai des Grands Augustins, the bookseller Pissot, another friend of Jefferson's, published *The General Advertiser,* a weekly gazette in English. Jefferson inserted American news to counteract the propaganda delivered by the London papers.

At 41, quai des Grands Augustins, one can browse, like Jefferson, in the Librairie "Les Neuf Muses" which was established on the same premises under the same name. Today, it deals in rare books and autographs.

One can fairly say that it was along the River Seine that Jefferson gathered the nucleus of the Library of Congress.

When the U.S. government moved from Philadelphia to the wilderness town of Washington, the legislature needed to have access to a collection of books. In 1800, John Adams approved an act of Congress founding the Library of Congress. In 1802, Jefferson, by then President, appointed his friend John J. Beckley as the first Librarian of Congress.

Unfortunately, in August 1814, British troops marched on Washington. They not only set fire to the Capitol and the White House, but also destroyed the 3,000 volume collection of the new Library.

By then retired to Monticello, Jefferson promptly offered to sell his personal library to Congress. The purchase was approved by only a slim majority of ten votes. Critics said that there were "too many works in foreign languages." Congress paid $23,950 for 6,487 books. They had been appraised at $3 for common size, $1 for very small books, and $10 for full-scale folios.

A great number of these books had been purchased in Paris along the River Seine. The Library of Congress adopted Jefferson's classification system; and despite the terrible fire of 1851, almost half of his collection still survives in the Library's Jefferson Fund.

After the sale, Jefferson, who had said, "I cannot live without books…," started a new library. When he died in 1826, over 1,000 new acquisitions were sold at auction.

RECHERCHES

HISTORIQUES ET POLITIQUES

SUR LES ÉTATS-UNIS

DE

L'AMÉRIQUE SEPTENTRIONALE,

Où l'on traite des établissemens des treize Colonies,
de leurs rapports & de leurs dissentions avec la
Grande-Bretagne, de leurs gouvernemens avant &
après la revolution, &c.

PAR UN CITOYEN DE VIRGINIE.

Avec quatre Lettres d'un Bourgeois de New-Heaven sur l'unité de la legislation.

PREMIÈRE PARTIE.

A COLLE,
Et se trouve A PARIS,
Chez FROULLÉ, libraire, quai des Augustins,
au coin de la rue Pavée.

---

1 7 8 8.

17

HOTEL DES MONNAIES

Franklin, Jefferson, Condorcet
11, quai de Conti, Paris 5e
METRO: Pont Neuf

The Royal Mint was brand new when Benjamin Franklin and Thomas Jefferson came to Paris. Completed in 1777 by an architect of humble origins, Jacques-Denis Antoine, the elegant simplicity of its facade on the quai de Conti captures the spirit of Louis XVI style.

Jefferson was interested in the production of coins and was a frequent visitor to the Mint. Before leaving for France in 1784, he had written *Notes on the Establishment of a Money Unit and of a Coinage for the United States.* In 1787, he watched a demonstration by a Swiss craftsman, Jean-Pierre Droz, who had invented a labor-saving machine capable of striking the two faces and the edge of a coin at the same time. Jefferson had hoped to hire Droz for the Philadelphia Mint, but plans never materialized. He remained, however, involved in the establishment of the U.S. Mint in Philadelphia.

The engraving and striking of commemorative medals was another function of the Royal Mint. When Congress voted to honor people who had taken part in the American Revolution, the medals were ordered at the Royal Mint. Benjamin Franklin supervised the engraving of the medal commemorating the surrender of Yorktown in 1782. Jefferson oversaw the creation of medals honoring Horatio Gates, Anthony Wayne, and John Paul Jones. The Royal Mint, itself, struck many medals having to do with the War of Independence including those honoring La Fayette, Franklin and the Treaty of Paris (chapter 9 page 42).

Today, modern coins are struck in Pessac, near Bordeaux, while the National Mint on the Quai de Conti continues to produce commemorative medals and collectors items. Medals commemorating Franco-American friendship as well as great events and prominent figures in American history are on display at the Mint Museum. George Washington, Abraham Lincoln and John F. Kennedy can be found along with many famous Americans at the Mint's Boutique.

The Hotel des Monnaies has yet another tie to American Independence. The Marquis de Condorcet, Inspecteur des Monnaies, resided here from 1777 to 1790. This famous mathematician was also one of the prominent political reformers of the Enlightenment. Jefferson came to know him well. In his *salon* overlooking the river, he and his brilliant and lovely young wife Sophie de Grouchy, hosted many friends of American Independence: Beaumarchais, La Fayette, Thomas Paine, and Thomas Jefferson.

Condorcet, who had understood the importance of the American Declaration of Independence, enjoyed discussing with its author his own proposals for a French Constitution. They did not agree on every point, however. Jefferson could not accept Condorcet's view that the "social contract" could be revised after each generation, nor was he concerned, like Condorcet, with the application of mathematics to political life.

The two men's esteem for each other, however, was mutual. Jefferson's library included not only some of Condorcet's scientific writings but works concerning America:

- *Lettre d'un Citoyen des Etats-Unis à un Français,* 1788.

- *Réflexions sur l'Esclavage des Négres,* first published in 1781 in Switzerland under the name of Joachim Schwartz.

- *De l'Influence de la Révolution d'Amérique en Europe,* 1786, which was dedicated to La Fayette "who at the age where ordinary men are hardly known in their own society deserves already the title of benefactor of two worlds."

In 1787, one of Ambassador Jefferson's most pleasant duties was to announce to Condorcet that he had been made a member of the American Philosophical Society (at the urging of Benjamin Franklin). (He had already been named honorary citizen of New Haven in 1785.)

Condorcet wrote to Jefferson as he was leaving Paris, "Monsieur Jefferson will always be the friend of the philosophers and of the free men of all countries." The two men continued to correspond during the French Revolution. When Condorcet felt that the Revolution that he had tried to guide was getting out of hand and would eventually take his life, he entrusted the care of his daughter to Jefferson. In his last will, he asked that she be raised "in love, liberty, equality, and in the republican mores and virtues." Condorcet, prosecuted during the Terror, went into hiding but was arrested and died in prison in March 1794, four months before the end of the Terror.

Museum open every day except Monday, 11 a.m. to 5:30 p.m. and 12 a.m. to 5 p.m. on week-ends. Guided visits to the workshops at 2:15 p.m. on Tuesday and Friday. Boutique (2, rue Guénégaud) open Monday through Friday from 10 a.m. to 6 p.m., Saturday from 10 a.m. to 1 p.m. and 2 p.m. to 6 p.m.

18

PALAIS DE LA LEGION D'HONNEUR

Hôtel de Salm
Jefferson, Trumbull, Bulfinch and L'Enfant
64, rue de Lille, Paris 7e
METRO: Solférino

In Jefferson's time, the elegant Hôtel de Salm was best viewed from the terrace of the Tuileries Garden on the other side of the Seine. Now largely hidden by trees along the river bank, its neo-classic architecture is best appreciated by walking around the block occupied by the palace.

The main entrance, a handsome colonnaded courtyard, can be found on the rue de Lille while the second facade with its gracious rotunda overlooks a garden on what is now Quai Anatole France.

The Hôtel de Salm was built for the Prince of Salm-Krybourg, the ruler of an independent enclave in eastern France which was part of the German Empire. The Prince spent most of his time in Paris, however, and decided to have a palace built here in the Faubourg Saint-Germain, which had become the chic residential area for the aristocracy in the eighteenth century. The Prince had already dilapidated his fortune by living in grand style. Although he didn't have much money left, he apparently had the best taste and knew how to bluff his way through! Pierre Rousseau, a little-known architect, built this masterpiece which was completed in 1787, just two years before the French Revolution.

Jefferson loved the Hôtel de Salm which was being built when he arrived in Paris in 1784, and he used to go every day to the Tuileries Garden just to enjoy its serene lines and classic symmetry. In March 1787, he wrote: "I was violently enamored of the Hôtel de Salm, and I was in the habit of going almost daily to the Tuileries to look at it. The woman who hired out chairs, inattentive to my passion, was never sufficiently obliging to put a chair there for me, so that, seated on the parapet and twisting my head so as to be able to see the object of my admiration, I generally left there with a crick in my neck!"

Jefferson was so enthusiastic that he wrote to Major L'Enfant, recommending him to use the Palace for inspiration. L'Enfant, after taking part in the War of Independence as a military engineer, settled in the United States where he redesigned New York's City Hall and planned the new Federal capital in Washington, D.C.

Jefferson also took his protegés, John Trumbull and Charles Bulfinch, to see the Hôtel de Salm. Trumbull was the son of the governor of Connecticut, who had stabled Rochambeau's horses for the winter during the War of Independence. Young Trumbull, also a veteran of the war, went afterwards to London to study painting with Benjamin West.

Jefferson invited him to make himself at home at the ambassador's residence on the Champs-Elysées. The thirty-year-old Trumbull, who became the great painter of the War of Independence, was already at work on "The Surrender of Cornwallis at Yorktown." During the winter of 1788, Rochambeau, Chastellux, de Grasse, Lauzun, Barras, and, of course, La Fayette all came to sit for their portraits at the Hôtel de Langeac. It was there, also, that inspired and guided by Jefferson, Trumbull made the preliminary sketch for "The Declaration of Independence" which is now at Yale University.

Bulfinch was a young architect from Boston, and just twenty-one years old. He, too, appreciated the Hôtel de Salm and admired Les Invalides (see chapter 23 page 87). Their influence can be seen in his later works: the Capitol in Washington, Massachusetts General Hospital in Boston, and University Hall at Harvard.

It is Trumbull's historical paintings which now hang in Bulfinch's rotunda at the Capitol.

When the French Revolution started, the Prince de Salm quickly became a "patriot." He set his subjects free and they voted to become part of the French Republic in 1793. All this notwithstanding, the Prince found himself on the way to the guillotine in 1794 (just before Robespierre).

During the Revolution, the Palace was used as a political club. In 1804, it was sold at auction and became the seat of the Order of the Legion of Honor created by Napoleón in 1802.

Today, the Palace also houses a museum retracing the history of the Legion of Honor as well as orders of chivalry down through the centuries. Insignias and decorations from all over the world are on display including the Order of Cincinnati, the Congressional Medal of Honor, and the Purple Heart.

In 1924, a copy of the Palace was built as a museum in San Francisco. It stands in Lincoln Park on a rise overlooking the Golden Gate Bridge.

Just next door to the Palace, a railway station was built in 1898. Today, it is the Musée d'Orsay.

Museum open 11 a.m. to 5 p.m. (closed Monday). Entrance 2, rue de la Légion d'Honneur, Paris 7e (across the street from the entrance to the Musée d'Orsay). Tel 01.40.62.83.83.

19

REVOLUTIONARY ASSEMBLIES

**Thomas Paine: The American delegate to the
National Convention
opposite 230, rue de Rivoli, Paris 1er
METRO: Tuileries**

A plaque on one of the columns of the gate to the Tuileries Gardens, opposite 230 rue de Rivoli, recalls that between 1789 and 1793, three Legislative Assemblies met here in the Royal Manège which has since been destroyed. The speaker of the Assembly sat on one of the long sides of the riding arena while delegates of the same political persuasion sat together either to his right or his left. For the first time, the words right and left took on political meaning.

It was here that the National Convention voted to abolish the monarchy and set up the first French Republic in 1792. One of the delegates was a famous American, Thomas Paine, who had been elected to the Assembly by four different constituencies.

An Englishman by birth, Paine had emigrated to America in 1774 where he eloquently took up the cause of independence. *Common Sense,* written in 1776, stirred the hearts and minds to action.

Paine first came to Paris in March 1781 to help secure more financial and military help from the French. The years just before the French Revolution saw Paine once more in Paris where he followed political events very closely. After the Bastille fell on July 14, 1789, La Fayette gave him the keys to bring to George Washington. They are still at Mount Vernon. On July

14, 1790, when everyone thought that the Revolution was over and all Frenchmen reconciled, Paine arrived at the Fête de la Fédération carrying the Stars and Stripes (see cover of this book).

★   ★

SUR CET EMPLACEMENT
Avant l'ouverture de la rue de Rivoli
s'élevait la salle du manège
ou siégèrent successivement:
L'ASSEMBLEE CONSTITUANTE
du 9 novembre 1789 au 30 septembre 1791
L'ASSEMBLEE LEGISLATIVE
du 1er octobre 1791 au 21 septembre 1792
LA CONVENTION NATIONALE
du 21 septembre 1792 au 9 mai 1793
et où fut instituée
LA REPUBLIQUE
le 21 septembre 1792

★   ★

Paine then returned to England where he wrote a reply to Edmund Burke who had severely criticized the Revolution in France. His pamphlet, *The Rights of Man,* published in March 1791, sold hundreds of thousands of copies. It made Paine so popular in France that he was given honorary French citizenship in August 1792 and elected to the National Convention the following month.

Elected while he was still in England, Paine arrived in Paris in time to vote at the first session. He was quickly appointed to a committee to draft a new constitution. Paine knew no French, but spoke English with Danton, Condorcet, and Brissot (chapter 22 page 84). When in session, his English-speaking friends would sit next to him and translate the proceedings.

Paine had many ideas that were ahead of his time: free education for all children, retirement at sixty, the right of workers to negotiate salaries and working conditions, relief for the aged and sick, a progressive income tax, the abolition of slavery and equality of the sexes.

At the end of 1792, sensing a more radical turn of events, Paine began to oppose the incipient terrorist policies of the Assembly. In virtue of his devotion to the ideas he upheld in the *Rights of Man,* he courageously pleaded against the death penalty for Louis XVI. He proposed rather that the King and his family be sent to exile in the United States where they could learn the meaning of democracy. Paine was turned down.

Although Paine was an American citizen, he was arrested and jailed on the order of the fanatical Robespierre for having defended the King. Taken to prison at the Luxembourg on December 28, 1793, he stayed there until November 5, 1794 when he was released thanks to the efforts of the new American Ambassador, James Monroe (chapter 21 page 89). While in prison, he continued writing *The Age of Reason* and finished it while a guest of Monroe's on rue de Richelieu.

Paine went back to the United States in 1802 but continued to be remembered by the French. Napoléon Bonaparte said that he was "the spirit to which a golden statue should be raised in every city in the world"

Although it is not solid gold, the French have raised a gilded statue to Thomas Paine across the street from 15, boulevard Jourdan, Paris 14e.

It says: THOMAS PAINE
       CITOYEN DU MONDE
       1737-1809
       ENGLISHMAN BY BIRTH
       FRENCH CITIZEN BY DECREE
       AMERICAN BY ADOPTION

20

LA CONCIERGERIE

**Revolutionary Prison
1, quai de l'Horloge, Paris 1er
METRO: Cité**

Once the royal palace of the medieval kings, the present Palais de Justice has been used as a law court since the fourteenth century. The quarters of the Concierge or keeper of the royal house were converted into a prison. La Conciergerie along with the guillotine recall perhaps the grimmest memories of the French Revolution. Here, as many as 1200 men and women were held before being taken to the Revolutionary Tribunal and—most often from there to the guillotine.

Destiny is such that many of those who fought for liberty in the United States were jailed here ten years later. Three great Frenchmen who fought for America in the War of Independence experienced the terrors of imprisonment in the Conciergerie.

Rochambeau:

After the victorious General of Yorktown returned to France in 1783 at age fifty-nine, he still did not retire. Louis XVI honored him with an appointment as commanding general of the most important military region, the North, where he spent four years at his headquarters in Calais.

In the summer of 1789, the clouds of the Revolution were gathering as Louis XVI ordered Rochambeau to calm popular uprisings in Alsace. He left Paris on the eve of July 14 to the sound of shots being fired in the streets.

In September 1790, he was sent back again to the North to re-establish discipline at a time when soldiers were getting involved in the politics of the Revolution. France's neighbors were mobilizing their forces to combat the spread of her ideas to their countries.

Rochambeau swore allegiance to the new constitutional monarchy in 1791. However, he was deeply troubled by his King's attempt to flee France as well as the exodus of military officers—émigrés as these aristocrats were called—who were leaving the army in droves. Determined to remain loyal to France and too good a soldier to "desert," Rochambeau stayed on to fight and defend the northern borders. For his courage, he was named Marshal of France.

In 1792, however, he asked to be relieved of his command and returned, at last, to his estate in Vendôme. News of his old friends continued to reach him as he heard that, one by one, they had either emigrated or gone to the scaffold. In April 1794, it was his turn. Rochambeau was arrested, taken to Paris, and imprisoned in the Conciergerie. It was only a miracle that he escaped the guillotine. Released six months later, after the fall of Robespierre, he returned home to enjoy thirteen years of peaceful retirement and the honors he so well deserved.

In 1803, Napoléon, then Emperor, invited Rochambeau to the Tuileries. He told the seventy-eight-year-old Marshal that the officers who had served under him in America made the best generals, starting with his Chief of Staff, General Alexandre Berthier.

Lauzun:

Head of the Cavalry and Commander of the Legion of Foreign Volunteers at Yorktown, Lauzun was sent to the guillotine in 1793, twelve years after bringing home the news of the allied victory. Lauzun had faithfully served his country when the Revolution started. He was first aide de camp in the North to

Rochambeau, his old commander from the American campaign.

Later, he was sent to Strasbourg to command the army in Alsace. He continued to serve as the Terror took over in France and as La Fayette tried to escape to Holland. No longer the Duc de Lauzun or the Duc de Biron, he called himself just Citizen General Biron. Another successful tour of duty saw him at the head of the army of the Alps in Nice before being sent to the Vendée to put down the popular uprising of the royalists against the Republic. Unfortunately, he was accused of being too humane. He was recalled to Paris and thrown into one of the revolutionary prisons. The prison was full of aristocrats and pretty ladies who had been part of his life. With his usual panache, the forty-six-year-old Lauzun found a way to lift everyone's spirits!

Called to the Revolutionary Tribunal, he identified himself as Cabbage, Turnip Biron, to make fun of the revolutionaries' new craze of replacing "so-called" saints names by non-religious names!

Condemned to death, he was taken to the Conciergerie to await execution. Determined to live his life to the end, he ate a copious snack of oysters and white Bordeaux wine before being led to the guillotine.

That was the style of a man who lived in the building which is now the Hôtel Ritz, on Place Vendôme.

Admiral d'Estaing:

Charles Henri, Comte d'Estaing, who had led the first French fleet to America in 1778, was taken to the Conciergerie in April 1794. Although he tried to serve the Revolution and managed to have his rank of Admiral confirmed by the revolutionary government, he also went from here to the guillotine at age 65.

When he reached the scaffold, d'Estaing said, "After you cut off my head, offer it to the English. You will get a good price!"

Conciergerie open 9:30 a.m. to 6:30 p.m. from April 1 to September 30. Open 10:00 a.m. to 5:00 p.m. from October 1 to March 31.

PALAIS DU LUXEMBOURG

**Prison for Thomas Paine, General O'Hara, Danton;
Barras' Residence
15, rue de Vaugirard, Paris 6e
Metro: Odéon**

Today, the home of the French Senate, the Palace was built by Salomon de Brosse in the early seventeenth century for Marie de Medicis, Henri IV's widow. A masterpiece of early French classical architecture, the palace was used by members of the royal family until Louis XVI's brother, the future Louis XVIII, fled France during the Revolution. Requisitioned as a prison during the Terror, it was mainly reserved for aristocrats and foreigners.

The Luxembourg held some 1000 prisoners during the time Thomas Paine was there. Every day some were taken to the guillotine. It is said that Paine escaped execution because the chalk cross marking the doors of the condemned had been placed on the inside of his door rather than on the outside. The jailers, coming during the night to take the prisoners to the scaffold, passed by Paine's door which was closed.

Paine remained in the Luxembourg from December 1793 to November 1794. In January 1794, members of the American community in Paris, moved by the terrible fate of one of their compatriots, pleaded for his release at the National Convention...but to no avail. The American Ambassador at the time, Gouverneur Morris, did little to help. Morris said he was unable to ascertain if Paine was American because he had been born in England. Furthermore, he felt no responsibility for him because Paine had accepted honorary French citizenship (along with Washington, Hamilton and Madison!) and had served in the French legislature.

James Monroe, when he arrived in Paris to replace Morris, had no such questions. Monroe wrote to Paine: "By being with us through our revolution, you are of our country absolutely as if you had been born there; and you are no more of England than every native American...To the welfare of Thomas Paine, the Americans are not, nor can they be indifferent." He did everything he could to have Paine released and was finally successful on November 5, 1794. Robespierre had been sent to the guillotine at the end of July, and this certainly helped.

While in prison, Paine found Danton, his colleague from the National Convention. Both men had worked on the same committee to draft a new constitution for the Republic. Meeting Paine, Danton said: "What you have done for the happiness and liberty of your country, I have in vain tried to do for mine. I have been less fortunate but not more guilty!" Unfortunately, Danton was guillotined before the end of the Terror.

There were other prisoners at the Luxembourg: Thomas Griffith of Baltimore and William Haskins of Boston. Paine also met General O'Hara, the very man who had surrendered Cornwallis' sword at Yorktown (chapter 7 page 38). Their sad state reconciled the American patriot and the British general who kindly asked his doctors to take care of Paine who suffered from a terrible fever. A Prussian, Anacharsis Cloots, who had, like Paine, been elected to the National Convention was also there. The guillotine prevented him from returning to his seat on the Convention as Paine did after his release from prison. Paine finished his term of office with dignity but was too disillusioned with the turn of events to seek re-election in October 1795.

The French Revolution which had brought Paine in

misery to the Luxembourg brought Barras in power and glory to the same place at the end of 1795.

Barras (or rather the Count de Barras) was an aristocrat and officer in the Pondichery regiment. His uncle, Louis Barras de Saint Laurent, had taken the French fleet in 1781 from Newport to the Chesapeake to join forces with de Grasse arriving from the West Indies and had participated in the battle of Yorktown. As the personal representative of de Grasse, he signed the surrender along with Washington and Rochambeau.

During the Revolution, his nephew managed to have people forget that he was an aristocrat. A delegate to the National Convention like Paine, he survived the Terror which ended with the downfall of Robespierre on July 27, 1794 (9 Thermidor according to the new calendar). A year later, under a new constitution, he became a member of the Directory, a more moderate government which succeeded the extremists of the Terror. Still a survivor, he was the only member of the Directory who stayed in power from the first to the last day of this new version of the Republic from 1795 to 1799.

During these four years, he was the strongman of France in charge of the Police and the Ministry of the Interior. That won him the nickname "King of the Republic." He resided at the Luxembourg Palace where he entertained lavishly and led a very dissolute life. One of his guests was Thaddeus Kosciuszko, the Polish patriot who had fought in the War of Independence and who had built the first fortifications at West Point.

Barras was finally thrown out of office by his former "protégé," Napoléon Bonaparte, who seized power in a coup d'etat on 18 Brumaire (November 9, 1799), and brought the French Revolution officially to an end.

Although entrance to the Luxembourg Palace, the home of the French Senate, is restricted, the outstanding gardens, both English and French style, are open daily to the public and are well worth the visit.

Nearby, a plaque on the building at 10, rue de l'Odéon recalls that Thomas Paine lived here from 1797 until his return to America in 1802.

★ ★

Thomas PAINE
1737-1809
Anglais de Naissance
Américain d'adoption
Français par Decret
a vécu dans cet immeuble de 1797 à 1802.
Il mit sa passion de la liberté au service de la
Revolution Française, fut député à la Convention
et écrivit *Les Droits de l'Homme.*
Lorsque les opinions sont libres, la force de la
vérité finit toujours par l'emporter.

★ ★

JACQUES-PIERRE BRISSOT'S RESIDENCE

1, rue de Gretry, Paris 2e
METRO: Quatre Septembre

Jacques-Pierre Brissot de Warville lived in this building from 1790 to 1793. His short but brilliant political career is symbolic of the profound influence of the American Revolution on those who played a leading role at the start of France's revolution. His admiration for America is indicative of the understanding and friendship that developed between French and Americans at that time.

Born into a middle-class family from Chartres, Brissot went to Paris to study law in 1774 but soon found his vocation as a professional writer and journalist. With the arrival of Franklin in 1776, he became fired with enthusiasm for the American cause and dreamed of how freedom and democracy could bring change to France as well.

He greatly admired Saint John Crèvecoeur whose vision of America in *Letters from an American Farmer* was not unlike his own. In 1787, he founded with Crèvecoeur "La Société gallo-américaine" to promote mutual understanding and the exchange of ideas and information between the two countries.

In 1786, the Marquis de Chastellux, who had served under Rochambeau in the War of Independence, published his *Voyages dans l'Amérique Septentrionale.*

Brissot immediately wrote a violent rebuttal accusing Chastellux of criticizing Quakers and belittling the Negroes. He wrote:

"There is no more difference between the nature of a modern man and that of ancient man than there is between the nature of a Negro and that of a white man...The dignity of man consists in his liberty, in his equality before the law,...in his subjection only to those laws to which he has given his consent, in the control he exercises over those to whom he has entrusted political authority..."[1]

A man of passionate commitments, Brissot founded the Society of Friends of the Blacks early in 1788. All the liberals of the time wanted to belong...La Fayette, Mirabeau, Abbé Grégoire, and Condorcet, who soon became President of the Society. Under his leadership, the Society's influence contributed to the decision to free the Blacks in the French colonies.

★   ★

**EN CETTE MAISON
HABITA EN 1793 LE CONVENTIONNEL
JACQUES PIERRE BRISSOT
1754-1793**

★   ★

In the summer of 1788, Brissot travelled to America. He tells us in his *Memoires*: "Indignant against the despotism under which France suffered, I travelled... to the United States of America, to learn there how to carry out in my own country a similar revolution, or else to settle there with my family if I had to abandon my hopes for such a revolution."[2]

He later published the account of his trip from Boston to Virginia called *New Travels in the United States of America.* His trip was cut short by the news that the Estates-General had been summoned in France. He quickly returned home to participate in the events that he had so eagerly awaited.

Brissot plunged into the fray, published a revolutionary newspaper in Paris, *Le Patriote Français,* and became a prominent leader of the legislative assembly and the National Convention. He was one of the leaders of the Girondin party—the group had previously been called the "Brissotins." With Condorcet, he was one of the first proponents of a republic in France. He also advocated going to war with all the monarchs of Europe to spread the Revolution and create other republics.

Finally, at the beginning of 1793, he felt that the revolution was going too far and voted against the death penalty for Louis XVI. This vote precipitated his fall from power and he, too was sent to the guillotine before the end of the year. At thirty-nine, Brissot died a victim of the revolution he had advocated and led.

[1] *Examen critique des Voyages…de M. le Marquis de Chastellux,* pp. 104-110

[2] *Mémoires II,* p. 275

HOTEL DES INVALIDES

France's Farewell to George Washington
Esplanade des Invalides, Paris 7e
METRO: Invalides or Latour-Maubourg

On a wide expanse west of Paris, Louis XIV decided to build an immense complex to house 3,000 invalid officers and soldiers who had served in his many wars.

The Hôtel des Invalides, built in the late seventeenth century by architects Libéral Bruant and Jules Hardouin Mansart, is a magnificent example of French classical architecture. Louis XIV could be justly proud of this masterpiece of urban planning—at once a barracks, retirement home, hospital, and monastery—with its own governor and its own clergy. Everything down to the silverware was designed according to a set plan.

Today, Les Invalides still houses nearly a hundred veterans. The Army Museum has taken over much of the inner courtyard, and, since 1840, Napoléon's tomb stands under the great dome of the church.

One of the first Americans to visit Les Invalides was Benjamin Franklin, who was looking for one of the great natural scientists of his time: Antoine-Augustin Parmentier. After a competitive exam, Parmentier had been appointed Pharmacist at Les Invalides where he worked with the doctors and sisters taking care of the soldiers. His great passion, however, was to solve the problem of frequent famines. Convinced that potatoes were the solution, he studied them and even grew them in a secret corner of the garden at Les Invalides. He finally won his battle against prejudice about this strange plant when the King and Queen decided to promote potato consumption by wearing potato flowers in their hats! After that, there was never a famine in France, and Benjamin Franklin knew a friend of mankind when he saw one.

When the news of George Washington's death arrived in France in January 1800, the officers of the French Army wore mourning, and flags were flown at half mast for ten days. The commanding general read the order of the day to the troops assembled in the courtyard of Les Invalides:

> "Washington is dead. This great man fought against Tyranny. His memory will always be cherished by the French people as by all free men of the two worlds, and especially by the French soldiers, who, like him and the American soldiers, fought for equality and liberty."

The author of this proclamation was General Napoléon Bonaparte.

A memorial service then followed in the church. General Bonaparte, First Consul at the time, presided as government officials and troops gathered to honor Washington, who had been made an honorary French citizen by the National Assembly in 1792. A funeral oration was given by the famous orator, Louis de Fontanes. General Lannes placed ninety-six flags captured by the armies of the French Republic in front of a bust of General Washington.

To this day Governors of Les Invalides are selected from among the generals renowned for bravery. Three of them had a connection with America:

- General Armand *Baville* was made governor in 1796. He had served as a sergeant in the Bourbonnais regiment and fought at Yorktown.

- Maréchal Jean-Baptiste *Jourdan,* governor in 1830, had served in America as a private during the War of Independence.

- Prince *Jérôme Bonaparte,* Napoléon's brother, became governor in 1852. While an officer in the French Navy, he met and married Betsy Patterson in Baltimore. He is the grandfather of Charles Bonaparte, US Secretary of the Navy (1905) and Attorney General (1906). His tomb stands in the first chapel to the left in the Dome Church.

The Musée de L'Armée has a Rochambeau room with mementos of the War of Independence.

Several Gribeauval cannons, which helped win the Battle of Yorktown, can be found displayed in the northeast gallery of the main courtyard.

Musée de l'Armée and Eglise du Dôme (Napoléon's Tomb) open from 10 a.m. to 6 p.m. (April 1st to September 30) and from 10 a.m. to 5 p.m. (October 1st to March 31st).

PLAQUE TRANSLATIONS

CHAPTER 3 P. 20 M.J.P.R.Y.G.D. La Fayette, Lieutenant General, Member of the Chamber of Deputies, born at Chavaniac, Haute Loire, on September 6, 1757, married on April 11, 1774, to M.A.F. de Noailles.

CHAPTER 3 P. 23 The meeting between General La Fayette and Queen Marie-Antoinette on his return from America took place in this building on February 15, 1779.

CHAPTER 3 P. 24 General La Fayette, defender of liberty in America, one of the founders of liberty in France, born on September 4, 1757 at Château Chavagnac in Auvergne, died in this building on May 20, 1834.

CHAPTER 4 P. 26 "I have not yet begun to fight" John Paul Jones, Captain of the United States Navy, Chevalier de l'Ordre du Mérite Militaire, and one of the heroes of the American War of Independence, died in this building on July 18, 1792.

CHAPTER 5 P. 29 Jean Baptiste Donatien de Vimeur, Comte de Rochambeau, Maréchal de France, 1725–1807, resided here when he was chosen to command the army sent by Louis XVI to America in 1780 to help the United States to win its independence.

The French chapter of the Society of Cincinnati was founded here, January 7-16, 1784, in memory of the American War of Independence.

CHAPTER 6 P. 33 In memory of the Comte de Grasse On January 16, 1788, the body of François-Joseph Paul de Grasse, Marquis de Tilly des Prince d'Antibes, Rear Admiral of the Navy, Commander of the Royal and Military Order of Saint-Louis, was buried in this church.

Knight of the Order of Saint-Jean de Jerusalem, Member of the Society of Cincinnati, born at Château du Bar, near Grasse, on September 13, 1722.

His naval victory over the English at Chesapeake on September 5, 1781, made possible the surrender of Yorktown, under siege by the French-American army commanded by General Washington and General Rochambeau. He thereby gained with them the everlasting glory of having ensured the independence of the United States of America.

May He Rest in Peace.
This commemorative plaque was placed here by the Society of Cincinnati of France on October 19, 1931, the 150th anniversary of the surrender of Yorktown and in memory of this military victory of immeasurable consequences.

CHAPTER 7 P. 39 Benjamin Franklin, 1706-1790, the genius who freed America and flooded Europe with light: the sage whom two worlds call their own.

CHAPTER 8 P. 41 La Fayette & Washington, Homage to France for its generous contribution to the struggle of the people of the United States for independence and liberty.

CHAPTER 9 P. 43 In this building, formerly the Hôtel d'York, David Hartley, in the name of the King of England, Benjamin Franklin, John Jay, John Adams, on behalf of the United States of America, signed the final peace treaty recognizing the independence of the United States on September 5, 1783.

CHAPTER 10 P. 46 Here stood an outbuilding of the Hôtel de Valentinois. From 1777 to 1785 it was the home of Benjamin Franklin, who had the first lightning rod built in France erected on it.

Presented by C.C. Charley to the Société Historique d'Auteuil et de Passy, 1910.

CHAPTER 11 P. 50 In this building, between August 1784 and May 1785, resided John Adams, the 2nd President of the United States, 1797-1801, and one of the founders of America's independence, and his son, John Quincy Adams, the 6th President of the United States, 1825-1829.

CHAPTER 12 P. 54 Here resided Thomas Jefferson, Minister of the United States in France, 1785-1789, President of United States, 1801-1809, author of the American Declaration of Independence, founder of the University of Virginia.

This plaque was placed here on April 13, 1919, by graduates of the University of Virginia who were soldiers in World War 1.

In commemoration of the centennial of the founding of the university.

CHAPTER 15 P. 64 Café Procope
Here, in 1686, Procopio dei Coltelli founded the age-old Café Procope and the most celebrated center of the literary and philosophical life of the 18th and 19th centuries. It was frequented by La Fontaine, Voltaire, the Encyclopedists, Benjamin Franklin, Danton, Marat, Robespierre, Napoleon Bonaparte, Balzac, Victor Hugo, Gambetta, Verlaine, and Anatole France.

CHAPTER 19 P. 75 On this site, prior to the opening of the rue de Rivoli, stood the riding school where met successively the Constituent Asembly from November 9, 1789, to September 30, 1791, the Legislative Assembly from October 1, 1791, to September 21, 1792, the National Convention from September 21, 1792 to May 9, 1793, and where the Republic was established on September 21, 1792.

CHAPTER 21 P. 83
Thomas Paine
1737-1809
Englishman by birth
American by adoption
French citizen by decree

Lived in this building from 1797 until 1802. His love of liberty served the cause of the French Revolution. He was elected member of the National Convention, and was the author of *The Rights of Man*. When opinions are expressed freely, truth wins.

CHAPTER 22 P. 85 Jacques Pierre Brissot (1754-1793), Member of the Convention, resided in this building in 1793.

BIBLIOGRAPHY

ALSOP, Susan Mary. : *Yankees at the Court*
The first Americans in Paris
Doubleday & Company—New York, 1982

ANTIER, Jean-Jacques. : *L'Amiral de Grasse, Vainqueur*
à la Chesepeake
Illustrations de Philippe Ledoux
Editions maritimes et d'outre mer—Paris, 1971

AZEAU, Henri. : *Complot pour l'Amérique (1775-1778)*
Le rêve américain de Beaumarchais
Editions Robert Laffont—Paris, 1990

BANCROFT, George. : *Histoire de l'action commune*
de la France et de l'Amérique pour l'indépendance
des Etats-Unis
Trois tomes
F. Vieweg, Libraire-Editeur—Paris, 1876

BIZARDEL, Yvon. : *Les Américains à Paris pendant*
la Révolution
Calmann-Lévy—Paris, 1978

BIZARDEL, Yvon. : *Les Américains à Paris sous*
Louis XVI et pendant la Révolution
En dépôt à la Librairie Historique Clavreuil—Paris, 1978

BOUCHER, François and HUARD, Frances Wilson.:
American Footprints in Paris
George H. Doran Company—New York, 1921

BRISSOT DE WARVILLE, Jacques Pierre. : *New Travels in the United States of America*
The Balknap Press of Harvard University Press — Cambridge, Massachusetts, 1964

BRISSOT DE WARVILLE, Jacques Pierre. : *Examen critique des Voyages dans l'Amérique Septentrionale de Monsieur le Marquis de Chastellux*
London, 1786

BRISSOT DE WARVILLE, Jacques Pierre. : *Mémoires (1754-1793) — étude critique et notes de Cl. Perroud*
A. Picard, 1911, 2 volumes

BUISSON, M. du. : *Abrégé de la Révolution de L'Amérique Angloise, depuis le commencement de l'année 1774 jusqu'au premier janvier 1778*
Cellot et Jombert Fils jeune — Libraires & Imprimeur — Paris, 1778

CASTRIES, Duc de. : *Le testament de la monarchie L'indépendance américaine (1774-1784)*
Librairie Arthème Fayard — Paris, 1958

CHARTRAND, Renè. : *The French Soldier in Colonial America*
Museum Restoration Service — New York

CHINARD, Gilbert. : *L'apothéose de Benjamin Franklin*
Imprimerie F. Paillart — Abbeville, 1955

CONDORCET. : *Lettre d'un Citoyen des Etats-Unis à un Français*
Philadelphia, 1788

CONDORCET. : *Réflexions sur l'Esclavage des Nègres (sous le nom de Joachim Schwartz), 1781*

CONDORCET. : *De l'Influence de la Révolution d'Amérique en Europe, 1786*

CONWAY, Moncure Daniel. : *Thomas Paine et la Révolution dans les Deux Mondes*
Plon — Nourrit et Cie — Paris, 1900

DAVIS, Burke. : *The campaign that won America — The story of Yorktown*
East Acorn Press, 1989

DAWSON, Warrington. : *Les 2112 Français Morts aux Etats-Unis de 1777 à 1783 en combattant pour l'indépendance américaine*
Société des Américanistes — Paris, 1936

FAY, Bernard. : *L'esprit révolutionnaire en France et aux Etats-Unis à la fin du XVIIIe siècle*
Librairie Ancienne Edouard Champion—Paris, 1925

FIECHTER, Jean-Jacques. : *Un Diplomate Américain sous la Terreur—Les années européennes de Gouverneur Morris—1789-1798*
Fayard—1983

FLEMING, Thomas J. : *Beat the last drum—The siege of Yorktown, 1781*
St. Martin's Press—New York—1963

FRIDDELL, Guy. : *Miracle at Yorktown*
Designed and Produced by Tom Hale
Davis Shockley & Partners, Inc.

HIGONNET, Patrice. : *Sister Republics—The origins of French and American Republicanism*
Harvard University Press
Cambridge, Massachusetts
London, England, 1988

JOHNSTON, Henry P. : *The Yorktown campaign and the Surrender of Cornwallis 1781*
Harper and Brothers—New York, 1881

KEMP, Alain. : *Yorktown*
Almark Publishing Co. Ltd.—London, 1976

LA LOGE d'AUSSON, Comte de. : *Yorktown ou Comment la France royale libéra l'Amérique*
Alexis Redier, Editeur—Paris, 1931

LASSERAY, Commandant André. : *Les Français sous les treize étoiles (1775-1783)*
Deux tomes
Imprimerie Protat Frères—Macon, 1935

LECOMTE, Solange et Daniel. : *Rochambeau*
Editions Lavauzelle—Paris-Limoges, 1976

MAUGRAS, Gaston. : *Les demoiselles de Verrières*
Calmann-Levy—Paris, 1890

MORTON, Brian N. : *Americans in Paris, An Anecdotal Street Guide*
The Olivia & Hill Press—Ann Arbor, Michigan, 1984

NASH, George H. : *Books and the Founding Fathers*
Library of Congress—Washington, 1989

NOAILLES, Vicomte de. : *Marins et Soldats Français en Amérique pendant la Guerre de l'Indépendance des Etats-Unis (1778-1783)*
Perrin et Cie, Libraires-Editeurs—Paris, 1903

RICE, Howard C. and Anne S.K. BROWN. : *Yorktown—Centenaire de l'Indépendance des Etats-Unis d'Amérique (1781-1881)*
Honoré Champion—Paris, 1886

RICE, Jr. Howard C. : *Thomas Jefferson's Paris*
Princeton University Press—Princeton, N.J. 1976

SAINT JOHN DE CREVECOEUR. : *Lettres d'un cultivateur américain adressées à Wm. S…. on Esqr. depuis l'année 1770 jusqu'en 1786*
Trois tomes
Cuchet Libraire—Paris, 1787

SALINGER, Pierre. : *La France et le Nouveau Monde*
Editions Robert Laffont—Paris, 1976

SYMONDS, Craig L. : *A battlefield Atlas of the American Revolution*
The Nautical & Aviation Publishing Company of America, Inc.—Baltimore, 1991

THOMAS, Williams S. : *The Society of the Cincinnati 1783-1935*
G.P. Putnam's Sons—New York, 1935

WALTER, Daniel. : *Gouverneur Morris Témoin de Deux Révolutions*
Imprimerie Merinat-Brive—Lausanne, 1982

INDEX

ACKNOWLEDGEMENTS

The authors
wish to thank for
their help:

Ann Barbaro
Gilbert Bodinier
Gary Breunig
Marcel Carpentier
Jean Castarède
Alexandre Jouve
Robert J. Korengold
Claire-Alix Lajoinie
Aude Moysan
Rachel Paul
John Peter
Christine Rippes
Suzanne Tréguier

Garamond, Didot, Bodoni, and Baskerville are among the most important names in typographic history.

In recognition of the distinguished French type designer Claude Garamond (1480-1561), the text of this book is set in Simoncini Garamond, adapted from the original cutting for use in contemporary technology.

Francois Ambroise Didot (1730-1804), and his two sons, Pierre (1761-1853), and Firmin (1764-1836), continued the established family tradition as French type designers, printers, papermakers, and publishers.

In 1785, Francois hired Benjamin Franklin Bache, one of the two grandsons of Benjamin Franklin, as an apprentice to Firmin.

Pierre was the chief rival and competitor of Bodoni. Firmin became the official printer for the French Academy in 1811, was elected to Parliament in 1827, and in 1830 was offered the full directorship of the Imprimerie Royale.

The company was located at 56 rue Jacob, the former Hôtel d'York, and the site of the signing of the Treaty of Paris. (chapter 9).

Giambattista Bodoni (1740-1813), established his famous press in Parma, Italy in 1768, and patterned it after the Imprimerie Royale. About 1791, Bodoni began printing with typefaces based on the designs of the Didots. He was honored with a pension by Napoleon, and a letter from Benjamin Franklin praising his work. The letter was widely circulated by Bodoni who believed Franklin was the president of the United States.

The display type used on the cover and title page is Bodoni.

John Baskerville (1706-1775), the great English type designer and printer, died in the year of the Boston Tea Party. Since no one in England was interested in buying his types, they were purchased by Caron de Beaumarchais, (see Chapter 1), taken to France, and first used in an edition of the complete works of Voltaire.

To continue this tradition of Franco-American cooperation, the type was composed in New York City, and the book was printed and bound in Paris.

Designed by Alvin Grossman

*"Nobody
ever leaves
Paris
but with a
degree
of
tristeness."*

— ABIGAIL ADAMS

Imprimé en France